Andrew Woods
Grace Romano

Oxford Grammar

Third Edition

Name: ____________________

Class: ____________________

OXFORD
UNIVERSITY PRESS

Contents

Topic 1: Nouns, pronouns and adjectives

Topic 2: Verbs, adverbs and phrases

Topic 3: Text cohesion and language devices

Topic 4: Sentences

Topic 5: Sentences and punctuation

Topic 6: Using grammar

Topic 7: Extension and enrichment

Topic 1: Nouns, pronouns and adjectives

Learning intention

We are learning to use a variety of nouns (naming words) and pronouns, and how to expand noun groups with adjectives and articles to add more precise, varied and engaging information about people, places and things.

Unit 1.1 Common nouns

Just kidding!

Why did the girl throw the butter out of the window?

She wanted to see the butterfly.

What did the grape say when the elephant stepped on it?

Nothing, it just let out a little wine.

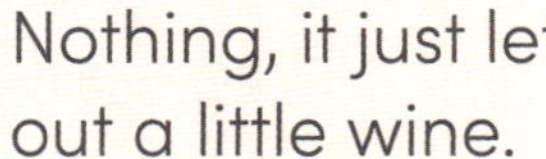

What did one plate say to the other plate?

Lunch is on me!

What sort of shoes do koalas wear?

Gumboots.

What did the tiger say when he saw a rabbit on a skateboard and a goat on a bike?

"Meals on wheels!"

Nouns name things. Common nouns name ordinary things. *Cat, chair, car, field* and *school* are all common nouns. A common noun only begins with a capital letter if it is the first word in a sentence.

1 Use the clues to write common nouns from the jokes.

- **a** spread me on bread ______________________
- **b** an animal with a trunk and big ears ______________________
- **c** something to wear on your feet in wet weather ______________________
- **d** a drink made from grapes ______________________
- **e** an insect ______________________
- **f** a female child ______________________
- **g** a striped wildcat ______________________
- **h** something you serve food on ______________________
- **i** a furry animal with a pouch ______________________
- **j** something to ride on and pedal ______________________
- **k** the second meal of the day ______________________
- **l** a flat platform with four wheels ______________________
- **m** an animal with long ears ______________________
- **n** a wall opening for light and air ______________________
- **o** a small, round fruit ______________________

Common nouns name everyday things.

2 Draw lines to match the nouns in Box A with the nouns in Box B to make three common nouns from the jokes page.

A	B
butter	board
skate	boots
gum	fly

Try it out!

On a piece of paper, write 26 **common nouns**, each beginning with a different letter of the alphabet.

Miss de Fyre's Amazing More Machine

Remember: Common nouns name ordinary things.
For example: *table, chair, hand, dog, box, baby*

Plural nouns are nouns that name more than one thing. (Plural means more than one.) For example: *tables, chairs, hands, dogs, boxes, babies*

When changing some nouns to plural, we add or change letters.

When Miss de Fyre puts one thing into her Amazing More Machine, more than one thing comes out the other end.

Miss de Fyre has put one box into her machine and many boxes have come out at the bottom.

To make some plural nouns we just add **s**.
For example: *one girl → many girls*   *a pencil → a box of pencils*

With nouns ending in s, x, sh, ch, ss and zz, add es to make them plural.
For example: **atlases, boxes, wishes, punches, classes, buzzes**

1 What will come out of Miss de Fyre's machine if she puts her toy elephant into it?

____

2 What will come out of Miss de Fyre's machine if she puts in these things?

a a log ______ **b** an egg ______ **c** a flower ______
d a clown ______ **e** a cup ______ **f** an apple ______

To make some plural nouns we add **es**.
For example: *one box → many boxes*   *a bush → lots of bushes*

3 Look at these plural nouns for the things that came out of Miss de Fyre's machine next.

- glasses
- dishes
- watches

Write the three things that Miss de Fyre had put into the machine.

a ______ **b** ______ **c** ______

4 Write the plural nouns for the objects that will come out of Miss de Fyre's machine if she puts in these things.

a a bush ______ **b** a patch ______ **c** a brush ______
d a dress ______ **e** a torch ______ **f** a bus ______

Try it out!

Write the names of two things you would like to put into Miss de Fyre's machine and the things that would come out.

in ______ out ______ in ______ out ______

Zoot Galoot – Alien visitor

The special names of people, places and things are proper nouns. Proper nouns begin with a capital letter.

Ricky, Abdul, America, Tasmania, Friday and *Grand Final* are all proper nouns.

When a **proper noun** has more than one important word, each word begins with a capital letter. For example: **Great Barrier Reef, New Zealand, Mr Clarkson, Melba Highway**

1 Read the comic strip about Zoot Galoot. Then answer these questions using proper nouns.

a What is the visiting alien's name? ______________________

b What is the alien's spaceship called? ______________________

c What is Zoot's robot called? ______________________

d Where does Zoot come from? ______________________

2 a Your teacher's name is a proper noun. Write your teacher's name.

____

b The name of the town, city or region in which you live is a proper noun. Write the name of the town, city or region in which you live. ______________________

c The name of your school is a proper noun. Write the name of your school. ______________________

(Did you remember to begin your proper nouns with capital letters?)

Here is Zoot Galoot's computer. ⟶

3 Zoot Galoot also has a name for his computer. Write a name that you think might suit Zoot's computer. ______________________

Try it out!

Writers sometimes choose **proper nouns** that suit the character, so that readers can picture what the character looks like.

a Draw lines to match the characters in Box A with the descriptions in Box B.

b Are the proper nouns in Box A or B? ______________________

A	B
Sleeping Beauty	A fast racehorse
The Wiggles	An unhappy character
Wonder Woman	Lively entertainers
Topsy Turvy Tom	A hero with amazing superpowers
Grumpy	A character who walks on his hands
Lightning	A pretty but tired princess
Eeyore (sounds like **heehaw**)	A donkey

The Noun Show

Howdy-doody everybody!
I have 12 NOUN cards below.
To be a winner, all you have to do is match the names on each NOUN card with the pictures on the next page!

victory	chair	gate	ladder
mountain	anger	gossip	fear
joy	road	strength	pencil

Nouns can be concrete or abstract nouns.
Concrete nouns are names for people, places, animals or things that we can see or touch.
For example: *car*, *man*, *school*, *kangaroo*
Abstract nouns name feelings, ideas or things we cannot see or touch.
For example: *peace*, *honesty*, *love*

1 Write the concrete nouns on Davey Dazzle's cards under the matching picture.

a 
____

b 
____

c 
____

d 
____

e 
____

f 
____

2 Write the abstract nouns on Davey Dazzle's cards under the matching picture.

a 
____

b 
____

c 
____

d 
____

e 
____

f 
____

3 Circle the abstract noun cards in "The Noun Show".

Try it out!

Circle the words that are **abstract nouns**.

horse beauty apple beach surprise sadness

Black Jack Mack

This is the fearsome and terrible pirate, Black Jack MacDonald.

Black Jack Mack rules the Seven Seas. He is King of the Waves. The oceans are his.

When Black Jack Mack sees a ship laden with treasure, he attacks it and sinks it.

Black Jack Mack captures the sailors on the ship and makes them walk the plank.

Last to be fed to the sharks is Captain Courageous. He trembles with fear. Black Jack Mack you are a cruel pirate!

However, when Mum comes in and pulls the plug on Black Jack Mack, he isn't quite so fearsome or terrible any more.

Pronouns are words that we can use in place of nouns.

For example: *Sam walked* ***her*** *dog around the block.* (We use *her* instead of *Sam* again.)

The bike skidded out of control and ***it*** *crashed into the fence.*

(We use *it* instead of using *the bike* again.)

Here are the pronouns that have been used in the story of Black Jack Mack.

I he mine his it them you

Using **pronouns** helps our writing flow because we do not have to repeat the same nouns.

1 Read "Black Jack Mack", then rewrite these sentences using pronouns in place of the people, places or things in bold.

a Black Jack Mack rules the Seven Seas. **Black Jack Mack** is King of the Waves. The oceans are **Black Jack Mack's**.

____

____

b When Black Jack Mack sees a ship laden with treasure, **Black Jack Mack** attacks **the ship laden with treasure** and sinks **the ship laden with treasure**.

____

____

c Black Jack Mack captures the sailors on the ship and makes **the sailors** walk the plank.

____

____

d Last to be fed to the sharks is Captain Courageous. **Captain Courageous** trembles with fear.

____

____

e When Mum comes in and pulls the plug on Black Jack Mack, **Black Jack Mack** isn't quite so fearsome or terrible any more.

____

____

Try it out!

Choose **pronouns** from the box that could replace the bold words.

a **You and I** are walking to school tomorrow. ______________

b **The tiger** growled at **Emma**. ______________

c **Barney** threw the ball. ______________

It
He
We
her

The Ogs of Od

The Ogs live in the Land of Od.

Some Ogs are big.
Some Ogs are small.

Some Ogs have long hair.

Some Ogs have short hair.

Some Ogs like soft, soppy music.

Some Ogs like cool dance music.

Most Ogs like loud music.

Some Ogs ride slow, spotty scooters.

Some Ogs drive fast red cars.

All Ogs love to swim in pools filled with thick, mushy, lumpy, green soup!

Some words **describe** or tell us more about nouns. These words are called adjectives.
He has red hair. She has an old dog. Today is wet and cold.

a Which word tells us more about his hair?

b Which word tells us more about her dog?

c Which words tell us more about today?

Adjectives tell us more about nouns. They can tell us about size, shape, number and colour.
The words **red**, **old**, **wet** and **cold** are adjectives.

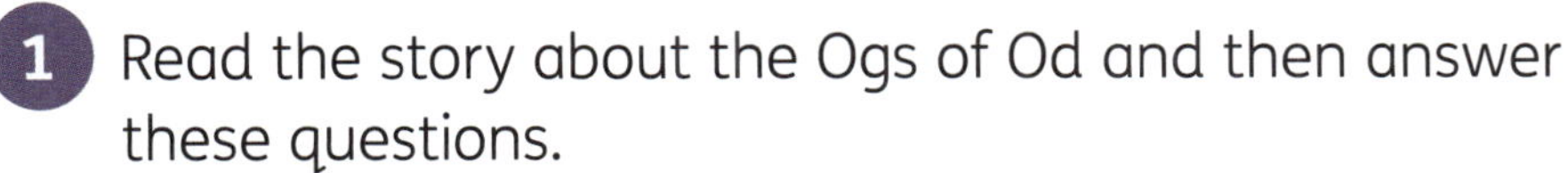

1 Read the story about the Ogs of Od and then answer these questions.

a Write the two adjectives in the story that **describe** the size of the Ogs.

________________ or ________________

b Write the two adjectives that **describe** the Ogs' hair.

________________ or ________________

c Write the five adjectives in the story that **describe** the sort of music Ogs like.

__________ __________ __________ __________

d Write the two adjectives that **describe** the cars that some Ogs drive.

____

e Write the adjectives that **describe** the sort of scooters some Ogs ride.

____

f Write the adjectives that **describe** the soup in the Ogs' swimming pools.

____

2 Underline the adjectives in these sentences.

a The desert was hot and dusty.

b The three black, savage dogs growled at the tall stranger.

c The funny clown was wearing a purple bow tie and a pointy hat.

d Elly could not fit the six square pegs into the round holes.

Try it out!

Write **adjectives** from the box that best match the nouns below.

six gusty slippery untidy tasty

a ____________ wind **b** ____________ room

c ____________ ice **d** ____________ sausages

Des Cripto

She smashes through heavy, wooden doors.

Terrible, savage monsters cannot stop her.

She crashes through solid brick walls.

She bends and breaks steel gates with her bare hands.

Nothing stops Desiree Cripto when it's home time.

OXFORD UNIVERSITY PRESS

Adjectives help us describe the characters and places in our texts. For example:
*The **quiet**, **thoughful** girl walked along the **windswept**, **deserted** beach.*
Character: *a **quiet**, **thoughful** girl*
Place (also called setting): *a **windswept**, **deserted** beach*

Adjectives are words that are used to describe nouns. For example:
They have bright, yellow coats. (**bright** and **yellow** are adjectives)

1 Write the adjectives from the comic strip that describe these nouns.

a The doors that Des Cripto smashes down ______

b The monsters that cannot stop Des Cripto ______

c The walls that Des Cripto crashes through ______

d Gates that Des Cripto bends and breaks ______

e Des Cripto's hands when she bends and breaks gates ______

Some adjectives can be made by adding endings to nouns.
For example: *wind + y = windy, wonder + ful = wonderful*

2 Write some of the adjectives from the box next to the characters they best describe. (The adjectives can be used more than once.)

a monster ______

b clown ______

c heroine ______

d prince ______

hairy noble brave
funny royal scary
horrible clever rich
handsome colourful
bold bad clumsy

3 In the space below, describe the place where one of the characters from question 2 lives. Use as many adjectives as you can in your description. Underline the adjectives.

______

______

Try it out!

Rewrite these nouns. Add **y** or **ful** to make **adjectives**.

a rain ______ **b** sand ______ **c** pain ______

d mess ______ **e** curl ______ **f** peace ______

An anvil for the blacksmith

Read this alphabet poem with your teacher.

An anvil for the blacksmith,
A bible for the preacher,
A chisel for a carpenter,
A desktop for the teacher.
An eggflip for the pastry cook,
A frigate for a sailor,
A gateway for the gardener,
And a hemline for the tailor.
An illness for a doctor,
A jetty for an angler,
A keyhole for the locksmith,
A lasso for the wrangler.
A mailbag for the postie,
A novel for a writer,
An opal for the miner,
And a punchbag for a fighter.
A queue for the shopper,
A rocket for the flyer,
A songbook for a singer,
A tune for the choir.
An upstairs for the butler,
A volleyball for the player,
A whistle for an umpire,
An X-ray of a patient.
A yawn from a baby,
A z or two for snoring,
And when I wake up after lunch,
My rhyme will be less boring.

The, *a* and *an* are called articles. We can use articles before a noun to make a noun group.
For example: ***the** blacksmith*, ***a** jetty*, ***an** illness*

1 Use the poem to help you write **the**, **a** or **an** before these nouns.

a	______ anvil	**b**	______ preacher	**c**	______ chisel
d	______ baby	**e**	______ illness	**f**	______ butler
g	______ opal	**h**	______ tailor	**i**	______ keyhole
j	______ bible	**k**	______ eggflip	**l**	______ teacher

We can add adjectives to make the noun group even more interesting.
For example: *an **angry** teacher, the **long** queue, a **brave** soldier*

2 Make interesting noun groups below by adding an article and an adjective.

a ______________________ sailor

b ______________________ rocket

c ______________________ apple

d ______________________ book

e ______________________ itch

f ______________________ monster

The means one particular thing, but **a** or **an** shows one of many things. For example: **Can you see the boy with blond hair? Can you see a boy with blond hair?**

3 Use articles to complete these sentences.

a Eight is ______ even number but nine is ______ odd number.

b Maya found ______ egg in ______ hen's nest.

c ______ ant is ______ insect but ______ spider is ______ arachnid.

Try it out!

We use the **article an** before most words beginning with a, e, i, o, u. However, some words beginning with u, eu and ew make a *yoo* sound (for example, *eucalyptus*). In those cases we use the **article a**. All other words also use the **article a**.
Write **a** or **an** before these words.

a	______ European car	**b**	______ unit	**c**	______ umpire
d	______ umbrella	**e**	______ unicorn	**f**	______ uniform

Miss Honey's cottage

Miss Honey has invited Matilda back to her little cottage for tea.

They came to a small green gate half-buried in the hedge on the right and almost hidden by the over-hanging hazel branches. Miss Honey paused with one hand on the gate and said, "There it is. That's where I live."

Matilda saw a narrow dirt-path leading to a tiny red-brick cottage. The cottage was so small it looked more like a doll's house than a human dwelling. The bricks it was built of were old and crumbly and very pale red. It had a grey slate roof and one small chimney, and there were two little windows at the front. Each window was no larger than a sheet of tabloid newspaper and there was clearly no upstairs to the place. On either side of the path there was a wilderness of nettles and blackberry thorns and long brown grass. An enormous oak tree stood overshadowing the cottage. Its massive spreading branches seemed to be enfolding and embracing the tiny building, and perhaps hiding it as well from the rest of the world.

from *Matilda* by Roald Dahl

1 Use "Miss Honey's cottage" to help you write common nouns to complete the following:

a a small green ______________________________

b a narrow ______________________________

c a grey slate ______________________________

d a tiny ______________________________

e the over-hanging ______________________________

2 Rewrite these common nouns as **plurals**.

a nettle ____________________ b window ____________________

c branch ____________________ d brick ____________________

Adjectives help to give a clearer picture of the story to the reader.

3 Use "Miss Honey's cottage" to write how the author Roald Dahl has used adjectives to help the reader picture Miss Honey's cottage.

a The oak tree was ______________________________ .

b Miss Honey's cottage was a ______________________________ cottage.

c The cottage had a ______________________________ roof.

d The oak tree had ______________________________ branches.

Try it out!

Rewrite the following sentences using the **pronoun it** where needed.

The cottage was tiny. The cottage was built with bricks that were old and crumbly, and the cottage looked like a doll's house.

____

____

____

____

____

____

Topic 1: Test your grammar

Nouns, pronouns and adjectives

1 Shade the bubble next to the **common noun**.

○ think ○ Ben ○ brain ○ laughing

2 Shade the bubble next to the correct **noun plural** for **church**.

○ churchs ○ churches ○ churchess ○ churchies

3 Shade the bubble next to the **proper noun**.

○ city ○ Hobart ○ town ○ street

4 Shade the bubble next to the word that is a **concrete noun**.

○ quick ○ school ○ thin ○ happiness

5 Shade the bubble next to the **abstract noun** that completes this sentence.

After killing the dragon, the warrior was rewarded for her ________ .

○ bravely ○ bravest ○ brave ○ bravery

6 Shade the bubble next to the **abstract noun**.

○ smile ○ happiness ○ giggle ○ chuckle

7 Shade the bubble next to the **noun** that would best match a character called Boppo.

○ clown ○ doctor ○ priest ○ teacher

8 Shade the bubble next to the word that best describes these **nouns**.

Robert, Australia, Atlantic, July

○ common ○ proper ○ abstract ○ concrete

9 Shade the bubble next to the word that best describes these **nouns**.

rectangle, triangle, pentagon, hexagon

○ common ○ proper ○ abstract ○ technical

10 Shade the bubble next to the **pronoun** from this sentence.

The bull was so strong that the farmer could not control him.

○ bull ○ was ○ strong ○ him

11 Shade the bubble next to the **pronoun** that would best replace the bold words in this sentence.

***Lily**, **Hannah** and **I** are going to the swimming pool today.*

○ They ○ We ○ Us ○ Them

12 Shade the bubble next to the **adjective** from this sentence.

The band was so loud I had to cover my ears.

○ band ○ loud ○ cover ○ ears

13 Shade the bubble next to the noun group that uses an incorrect **article**.

○ the apple ○ the apples ○ a apple ○ an apple

14 Circle the **noun groups** in the text below.

A mighty lion was asleep in the jungle. A cheeky, little mouse climbed onto the lion's back. The lion woke up. The terrified mouse hid behind a large, green fern.

How am I doing?

Colour the boxes if you understand.

Common nouns name ordinary things. ☐

Proper nouns are the special names of people, places and things. They begin with a capital letter. ☐

Concrete nouns name things that can be seen or touched. ☐

Abstract nouns name things that cannot be seen or touched. ☐

Pronouns are words that can take the place of nouns. ☐

Adjectives describe nouns. ☐

Topic 2: Verbs, adverbs and phrases

Learning intention

We are learning to identify and use verbs (action words), adverbs (words that describe how actions are done), and phrases (groups of words that work together) to make our writing more interesting and descriptive.

Unit 2.1 Doing verbs

The big game – Ogs vs Ugs

The Mighty Ogs run out onto the field.

The umpire bounces the ball. Big Toddy Og taps the ball to tiny Tommy Og.

Tommy sprints with the ball. He passes to Terri Og.

Terri catches the ball and she kicks it quickly.

The ball lands near Timmy Og. He picks it up.

Timmy dodges and weaves around the Ug defenders.

He boots the ball through the goal posts. Timmy turns to celebrate.

The Ug players laugh. Oops! Wrong end! Score = Ugs 1 Ogs 0.

Coach Olly Og tears out his hair.

Some words tell us what is happening or what someone is doing. Words that tell us what someone is doing are called doing verbs. Every sentence must have at least one verb.

For example: *He **plays** with the kitten. She **walks** to the shop.*

1 Read the story about the big game. Write the missing doing verbs.

- **a** What do the Mighty Ogs do? They ______________ out onto the field.
- **b** What does the umpire do? He ______________ the ball.
- **c** What does big Toddy do? Big Toddy ______________ the ball.
- **d** What does tiny Tommy do? He ______________ with the ball and then he ______________ the ball to Terri Og.
- **e** What does Terri Og do? She __________ the ball and then __________ it.
- **f** What does the ball do? The ball ______________ near Timmy Og.
- **g** What does Timmy Og do? Timmy ______________ the ball up. Timmy __________ and __________ around the Ug defenders. Timmy ______________ the ball through the goal posts.
- **h** What do the Ug players do? The Ug players ______________ .
- **i** What does Coach Olly Og do? He ______________ out his hair.

2 Choose a doing verb from the box that would best complete these sentences.

- **a** The Ogs ______________ onto the football field.
- **b** He ______________ towards the goal posts.
- **c** They ______________ striped jumpers.
- **d** The coach ______________ his own hair.

pulls
run
kicks
wear

Try it out!

Circle five **doing verbs** below that tell us what you can do in the playground at lunchtime.

run chase sit stand fly skip kick swim eat write drink climb

grow draw catch melt play sink dig explode disappear read

A dark and stormy night

It was a dark and stormy night.

Two large, mean dragons and a small, timid dragon sheltered in a cave. The two large, mean dragons turned to the smaller dragon.

"Tell us a story or we'll toss you out!" they growled. Quaking with fright, the timid dragon began his story.

"It was a dark and stormy night," he whispered. "Two large, mean dragons and a small, timid dragon sheltered in a cave. The two large, mean dragons turned to the smaller dragon."

"Tell us a story or we'll toss you out!" they grumbled. Quaking with fright, the timid dragon began his story.

"It was a dark and stormy night," he whimpered. "Two large, mean dragons and a small, timid dragon sheltered in a cave. The two large, mean dragons turned to the smaller dragon."

"Tell us a story or we'll toss you out!" they shouted. Quaking with fright, the timid dragon began his story.

"It was a dark and stormy night," he sighed. "Two large, mean ..."

Traditional tale

Some verbs tell us the way someone is talking. These verbs are called saying verbs. We can get to know characters in stories better through the way they speak.

For example: *The dragons* ***growled****. "That's funny!" the children* ***giggled****.*

1 Read "A dark and stormy night". Which three saying verbs tell us the way the small dragon spoke?

a w ______________________ **b** w ______________________

c s ______________________

2 Which three saying verbs tell us the way the two large dragons spoke to the small dragon?

a g ______________________ **b** g ______________________

c s ______________________

3 Use saying verbs from the box to complete these sentences.

groaned	whispered	laughed	asked
screamed	ordered	squealed	boasted

a "That's so funny," ______________________ Briana.

b "Oh no! Not Maths again," ______________________ the children.

c "Where do you live?" ______________________ Mr Fernandes.

d "Look out! It's going to hit you!" ______________________ Sandeep.

e "Ssh or she will hear us." ______________________ Luisa.

f "Please keep to the left," ______________________ the police officer.

g "I just saw a kangaroo in our front yard!" ______________________ my little brother with delight.

h "I scored the most runs ever!" ______________________ my cousin.

Try it out!

On a piece of paper, write your own sentences using these **saying verbs**.

- yelled
- giggled
- asked
- shouted
- begged

Unit 2.3 Thinking and feeling verbs

The Ogs at school

Toddy Og believes in UFOs.

Danny Og imagines dragons in days of old.

Tammy Og hopes the swimming pool is open.

Some verbs tell us about the way we think and feel.
These verbs are called thinking and feeling verbs.
For example: *I **think** fruit is good for you. We **love** playing outside.*

1 Read "The Ogs at school", then underline the thinking or feeling verbs in the sentences below.

a Tilly Og enjoys her Ogomobile on weekends.

b Ollie Og wonders why Ogs have to go to school.

c Tammy Og hopes the swimming pool stays open late tonight.

d Toddy Og believes in UFOs.

e Teddy Og decides on a Carrot Icy Blast for his after-school treat.

2 Write thinking or feeling verbs to complete the sentences below.

a Danny Og ______________________ dragons in days of old.

b Mr B Og ______________________ that none of the Ogs are paying attention.

3 Circle the thinking or feeling verb in the following sentences.

Alice noticed a large, red toadstool growing nearby. She wondered why it was such an unusual colour.

4 Look at question 3. In the thought bubble, write what Alice was thinking. Use thinking and feeling verbs to describe her thoughts.

Try it out!

Write your own sentences, using these **thinking** or **feeling verbs**.

wish remember know need

____

____

____

____

Billy Bud

Billy Bud washed his hair before he went to bed,
But Billy Bud used Green-Gro from his Daddy's shed.
Well foolish Billy has no hair upon his silly head,
For now he has a garden growing there instead.
Pretty little primroses growing in a row,
Daffodils and jonquils put on a lovely show.
Then there is a vegie patch to hoe, hoe, hoe,
And of course the grassy lawn which Billy needs to mow.

AjW

'Being' or 'having' words are called relating verbs.
The most common relating verbs are: *am, is, are, was, were, has, have, had*.

1 Read the poem about Billy Bud and then use relating verbs from the box to fill the gaps in the sentences.

am   is   are   was   were   has   have   had

- **a** Billy __________ no hair upon his head.
- **b** There __________ a vegie patch over there.
- **c** Billy __________ naughty to go into Daddy's shed.
- **d** There __________ primroses growing in a row.
- **e** __________ you ever been foolish like Billy?
- **f** Daffodils and jonquils __________ flowers.
- **g** Daddy saw that Billy __________ a garden growing on his head.
- **h** "I __________ a foolish boy," said Billy.

2 Use relating verbs from the box in question 1 to fill the gaps in Karli's "School Garden Report".

School Garden Report by Karli Tonetti

In our school we __________ a lovely garden. Part of the garden __________ filled with flowers and shrubs. Some of the flowers __________ fragrant. We also __________ a large kitchen garden. I __________ in charge of the herb section. This year, our school __________ awarded a certificate for the Best Kitchen Garden. We __________ all very proud of our garden.

Try it out!

Circle the **relating verbs** in these sentences.

- **a** "Ogs Ahoy!" is a funny story about the adventures of Toddy Og.
- **b** Bees have a very important role to play in pollinating plants.
- **c** Molly and Ravi are the fastest runners in Year 3.

Cooky's diary

Tuesday

On Tuesday, Cooky prepared for her TV cooking show by writing down what she was going to do.

I will need two eggs, some milk, some butter and two pieces of bread.

I will mix the eggs, milk and butter in a bowl.

I will pour the mixture into my frying pan and I will cook it slowly until the eggs are fluffy.

I will toast the bread.

When my eggs are ready, I will put them on the toast and serve them.

Wednesday

On Wednesday, it was time for Cooky's show. She explained to the viewers what she was doing as she prepared her meal.

First, I am getting two eggs, some milk and some butter from the fridge. Now, I am cutting two pieces of bread ready for toasting.

I am mixing the eggs, milk and butter in a bowl.

I am pouring the mixture into my frying pan and I am cooking it slowly until the eggs are fluffy.

Now that my pieces of bread are toasted, I am putting the eggs on them.

Yummm! They taste great.

Thursday

On Thursday, Cooky thought that she had better jot down in her diary what she had done on the show the night before. Here is what she wrote.

First I took two eggs, some milk and some butter from the fridge.

Then I broke the eggs into a bowl and added the milk and butter. I mixed them up and then I poured them into my frying pan.

I cooked the mixture slowly.

When my bread was toasted, I served up the eggs and ate the lot. My scrambled eggs were delicious.

Verbs can tell what happened then (in the past). For example: *Yesterday, I **watched** the game.*
Verbs can tell what is happening now (in the present). For example: *I **am watching** the game.*
Verbs can tell what will happen later (in the future). For example: *Tomorrow, I **will watch** the game.*

1 Read "Cooky's diary", then write whether the following sentences tell what has happened (past), what is happening (present) or what will happen (future).

a I am getting my eggs out of the fridge. ______

b I cooked the mixture slowly. ______

c I took some milk from the fridge. ______

d Now I am mixing the eggs, milk and butter. ______

e When I have mixed the eggs, milk and butter I will pour them into a frying pan.

______

f I will need eggs, milk and butter. ______

2 a Write a sentence about something you did yesterday. Underline the verb(s).

Yesterday, I ______.

b Write a sentence about something that you are doing now. Underline the verb(s).

I am ______.

c Write a sentence about something you will do tomorrow. Underline the verb(s).

Tomorrow, ______.

3 Choose from these verbs/verb groups to write three sentences – one sentence about the past, one sentence about the present and one about the future.

Past	Present	Future
played	are playing	will play
have written	am writing	will write
visited	is visiting	will visit

______

______

______

Try it out!

Make a prediction! On a piece of paper, write three sentences to say what you may be doing in a week's time, on this day next year and when you are an adult.

I must remember!

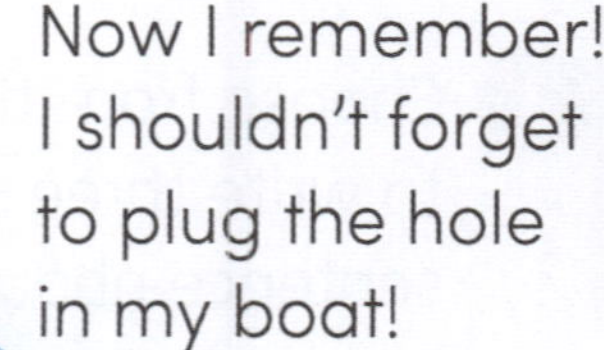

Some verbs are helping verbs. They are always used with another verb. Sometimes they tell how sure we are about doing something. They are called modal verbs.

will, can, shall, must are modal verbs we use when we are sure: *I* ***must*** *go.*
might, could, should, may are modal verbs we use when we are not sure: *I* ***might*** *go.*

Modal verbs are helping verbs. They are always used with another verb.

1 Read the comic strip "I must remember!" Write the missing modal verbs used as helping verbs in each sentence.

a "There's something I __________ remember," said Taddy Og.

b "I know there's something I __________ remember," said Taddy Og.

c "What was that thing I __________ forget?" wondered Taddy Og.

d "I __________ forget to plug the hole in my boat!" sighed Taddy Og.

2 Rewrite each of these sentences. Replace the modal verb (in bold) with a different modal verb so the writer sounds really sure about doing something.

a I **might** go to the movies.

____

b My friend Jack **may** come with us.

____

c We **could** take more care when crossing busy roads.

____

d I **should** clean my room this weekend.

____

Try it out!

Choose **modal verbs** from the box and write them in the gaps to help show how sure the writer is about each of the verbs in bold.

a I __________ **watch** a movie tonight.

b Tess __________ **catch** with both hands.

c We __________ **hurry** or we __________ **miss** the bus.

d You __________ **brush** your teeth after every meal.

should
will
might
can

The adventures of Adverb Man

Adverbs add details about verbs.

Adverbs often answer the questions: How? When? Where?

Many adverbs end in **-ly** (*quickly, silently, happily, carefully*) but some don't (*yesterday, now, there, fast*).

For example: *He walks* ***slowly***. (How does he walk? ***slowly***)

She knew ***immediately***. (When did she know? ***immediately***)

They stopped ***here***. (Where did they stop? ***here***)

Adverbs can be used to give clues about what a character is doing. For example: **powerfully, bravely, quickly**

1 Use the comic strip "The adventures of Adverb Man" to write one adverb to answer each of these questions.

a How does Adverb Man fly to the rescue? ______

b How does Adverb Man lift the evil monsters? ______

c How does Adverb Man fight? ______

d How do the bad guys tremble? ______

2 Use adverbs from the comic strip that add details about the verbs in bold.

a a bird **flying** ______ **b** a plane **soaring** ______

c a crowd **cheering** ______ **d** a hero **rescuing** ______

Adverbs can be added to verbs to make our opinion stronger when we are talking about a story or film.

For example: *I like Adverb Man. I* ***really*** *like Adverb Man.*

Adverbs can be added to adjectives to make our opinion stronger.

For example: *Adverb Man is fantastic! Adverb Man is* ***so*** *fantastic!*

Modal adverbs can be used to show how sure we are about something.

For example: *I would* ***probably*** *go to see the movie again. I would* ***definitely*** *go to see the movie again.*

3 Use the adverb ***very*** to write your opinion of Adverb Man.

______

______

______

Try it out!

Write **adverbs** to answer these questions.

a How might a spider crawl? ______

b How might an injured person stagger? ______

The monkey and the crocodile

Read the story about the monkey and the crocodile with your teacher.

Once, a monkey lived in a great tree by a river. In the river were savage crocodiles.

One day, the King Crocodile said to a smaller crocodile, "See that monkey in the treetop; I want to eat his heart. Get him for me."

The smaller crocodile thought about how he could catch the monkey. "I do not travel on the land and the monkey will not travel in the water. I will have to play a trick on him."

The crocodile swam until he was under the tree.

"Oh, Monkey!" he called. "There is some juicy ripe fruit on the island in the middle of the river. Why don't you go and get some?"

"Don't be silly, Crocodile," said the monkey. "I cannot swim."

"I will take you on my back," said the crocodile with a smile.

The greedy monkey wanted the fruit, so he jumped onto the back of the crocodile and off they went.

When the crocodile had reached deep water, he suddenly dived. The monkey was frightened. He did not like going under the water.

When the crocodile came up again the monkey spluttered "Why are you trying to drown me?"

"I am going to kill you and give your heart to my king," said the crocodile.

"Why Crocodile, if I'd known you wanted my heart, I would have brought it with me but I've left it in my treetop. If you want it, we could go back and fetch it."

The stupid crocodile agreed to take the monkey back to the tree to fetch his heart.

Of course, as soon as they had reached the shore, the monkey scampered up into the treetop. From the safety of his tree the monkey called down to the crocodile, "Nyahh! Nyahh! Stupid Crocodile! If you want my heart then you will have to climb my tree to get it!"

And with that the crocodile knew that he had been tricked by Monkey and both of them had learned important lessons.

A phrase is a small group of words without a verb.
For example: *in the tree, on the land, under the bridge, over here!*
Phrases can add details about how, when or where.

1 Use the phrases in the box to answer the following questions about the story.

to his king	in a great tree
in the middle of the river	on the land
by a river	on the island
on the crocodile's back	under the water

a Where did the monkey live? ______

b Where was the great tree? ______

c Where couldn't the crocodile travel? ______

d Where was the juicy, ripe fruit? ______

e Where was the island? ______

f How did Monkey travel across the river? ______

______

g Where did the crocodile dive? ______

h Where was Crocodile going to take Monkey's heart? ______

2 Use phrases to answer the following questions about your school.

For example: *Where is your teacher?*
out the front, at her desk, at home sick, in the staffroom, etc.

a Where is the clock? ______

b Where do you sit? ______

c Where do you keep your pencils? ______

d Where do you eat lunch? ______

Try it out!

Jokes and riddles are often answered with **phrases**.
Can you match these jokes and the **phrases** that are the answers?

Where did the King keep his armies?	**with a laser blade**
How does a robot alien shave?	**with their mountaineers**
How do mountains hear?	**up his sleevies**

Ramadan Moon

As the month of Ramadan approaches,
We search the sky for a sign.
Waiting,
Anticipating,
That silver sliver of brightness,
The shining white crescent
That is the Ramadan Moon.
And when the new moon is seen,
What wonderful excitement.
The news spreads like wildfire
Through cities, towns and villages,
Across deserts and grassland,
Into each and every home.

And Muslims of every nation,
Of every age and every hue
Will join the celebration
Of the arrival of the moon. "It's here. Ramadan is here,
The Month of Mercy has begun!"

Na'ima B. Robert

During Ramadan, the holy month of fasting in the Muslim calendar, Muslims only eat and drink after sunset: they fast during daylight hours.

The festival of Eid al-Fitr follows Ramadan. People celebrate with gifts and family parties, visiting friends, wearing new clothing and painting with henna. They also give money to the poor.

OXFORD UNIVERSITY PRESS

1 Underline the **verbs** in each of these sentences.

a Muslims celebrate Eid al-Fitr after Ramadan.

b During Eid al-Fitr people happily visit each other.

c Everyone loves the delicious treats on the table.

d "It's Eid al-Fitr!" shouted the children excitedly.

2 Use **adverbs** from the box to fill the gaps in these sentences.

happily hungrily generously tomorrow

a The children gobbled up the treats ______________________.

b Ramadan will end ______________________ and Eid al-Fitr will begin.

c We visit each other ______________________.

d Aisha's family ______________________ donate money to help poor people.

3 Underline the **phrases** in these sentences.

a Wonderful treats were set upon the table.

b Muslims do not eat or drink during daylight hours.

c Sheer khurma is a pudding cooked in sweet milk.

d During Ramadan, Muslims give money to the poor.

Be careful where you place a **phrase** in a sentence. Can you see why these sentences might confuse a reader? **She gave a box to the teacher that was made of metal. The dog gnawed the bone with sharp teeth.**

Try it out!

Write **modal verbs** from the box in these sentences.

might should will

a Ramadan is often at the start of autumn in Australia, so the weather ______________________ be quite mild.

b Aisha and her family ______________________ celebrate Eid al-Fitr every year.

c The children are excited that they ______________________ see wonderful treats on the table.

Topic 2: Test your grammar

Verbs, adverbs and phrases

1 Shade the bubble below the **doing verb** in this sentence.

Maggie walked to the shops before breakfast.

2 Shade the bubble next to the word that is a **doing verb**.

- ○ she
- ○ drank
- ○ glass
- ○ milk

3 Shade the bubble next to the **saying verb**.

- ○ thought
- ○ caught
- ○ cried
- ○ could

4 Shade the bubble next to the **saying verb** that would best complete this sentence.

"That's the funniest joke I've heard all day," ______ *Ruby.*

- ○ shouted
- ○ asked
- ○ screamed
- ○ chuckled

5 Shade the bubble next to the **thinking** or **feeling verb**.

- ○ played
- ○ does
- ○ wished
- ○ laughed

6 Shade the bubble below the **thinking** or **feeling verb** in this sentence.

We like the colour of our new car.

7 Shade the bubble below the **thinking** or **feeling verb** in this sentence.

Tom remembered that his homework was due on Friday.

8 Shade the bubble below the **verb** in this sentence.

The train arrived at the railway station.

9 Shade the bubble below the **relating verb** in this sentence.

My book has a lot of exciting chapters.

○ ○ ○ ○

10 Shade the bubble next to the sentence that describes something that happened in the past.

- ○ We rode our horses along Simpson's Lane.
- ○ We will ride our horses along Simpson's Lane.
- ○ We are riding our horses along Simpson's Lane.
- ○ We are going to ride our horses along Simpson's Lane.

11 Shade the bubble next to the words that form the **verb** in this sentence.

We might catch an early train to the city.

○ We might ○ might catch ○ an early ○ to the city

12 Shade the bubble next to the **adverb**.

○ lifts ○ beautiful ○ hero ○ bravely

13 Shade the bubble next to the **phrase**.

○ in the tree ○ am running ○ will play ○ are smiling

How am I doing?

Colour the boxes if you understand.

- Verbs can be doing, saying, thinking or feeling words. ☐
- Some verbs are "being" or "having" words. ☐
- Verbs can tell us when things happen. ☐
- Adverbs tell us more about verbs. ☐
- Phrases are small groups of words without a verb. ☐

Topic 3: Text cohesion and language devices

Learning intentions

We are learning to write antonyms and synonyms, and to use prefixes to make our writing more interesting and descriptive.

We are learning about paragraphs and how a topic sentence introduces the main point in a paragraph.

Unit 3.1 Text cohesion – Antonyms

The great Anto Nym

Anto Nym is one of the famous Nym Brothers. He is a circus acrobat.

Today he is going to walk the tightrope.

Anto Nym comes inside the circus tent and starts his act by saying hello.

He begins to climb up a high ladder.

When he is at the top, the bright lights go dim. A spotlight shines on Anto. He takes his first step forwards. Everybody is quiet. Nobody makes a sound.

When Anto Nym reaches the middle, he slips. The crowd cries in horror. Anto is in great danger, for there is no net. He grabs the rope and swings back up onto his feet.

He bows comically to the crowd.

The crowd laughs and gives him loud applause.

When Anto takes his last step and reaches the safety of the other side, there is more clapping and cheering. He climbs down the ladder.

Anto finishes his act by waving goodbye to the crowd. He walks backwards and goes outside where his brothers, Syno and Hommy, are waiting to perform.

Some words have opposites. These are called antonyms.
For example: *tall* and *short*, *back* and *front*, *day* and *night*, *shut* and *open*

Antonyms are opposites. Sometimes, a prefix can be added to the beginning of a word to give it the opposite meaning.

1 Read the story about Anto Nym and find the words that are antonyms for these words.

a up ____________ **b** first ____________
c hello ____________ **d** inside ____________
e starts ____________ **f** bright ____________
g cries ____________ **h** quiet ____________
i forwards ____________ **j** comes ____________
k danger ____________ **l** everybody ____________

2 Write words from the box that are antonyms of these words.

straight thin defend sunset weak old love stale buy steep

a thick ____________ **b** sell ____________
c strong ____________ **d** flat ____________
e young ____________ **f** attack ____________
g fresh ____________ **h** hate ____________
i bent ____________ **j** sunrise ____________

Sometimes we can add a prefix to the start of a word to make an antonym (opposite). Some common prefixes are *un-*, *dis-*, *im-* and *in-*.
For example: *un* + *happy* = *unhappy* (*happy* and *unhappy* are opposites)
dis + *like* = *dislike* (*like* and *dislike* are opposites)

3 Add the prefixes *un* or *dis* to these words to make antonyms.

a ________ appear **b** ________ real **c** ________ kind **d** ________ do
e ________ honest **f** ________ friendly **g** ________ fair **h** ________ lock
i ________ agree **j** ________ dress **k** ________ tie **l** ________ obey

Try it out!

Add a **prefix** to these words to make them **antonyms**.

a ________ possible **b** ________ safe **c** ________ connect
d ________ direct **e** ________ twist **f** ________ visible

Syno Nym the acrobat

Some words have the **same or nearly the same meaning** as other words. These words are called synonyms. For example: In the story, *jumps* could be replaced with *leaps* or *springs*.
Runs could be replaced with *races* or *hurries*.

1 Find words in the story about Syno Nym that are synonyms for these words.

a twirls ______________________ **b** vanishes ______________________

c enters ______________________ **d** awaits ______________________

e yelling ______________________ **f** incorrect ______________________

g audience ______________________ **h** sprints ______________________

i expands ______________________ **j** prepared ______________________

2 Draw lines to match the words in Box A with their synonyms in Box B.

A claps slides flexes flies more jumps

B soars bends applauds extra glides vaults

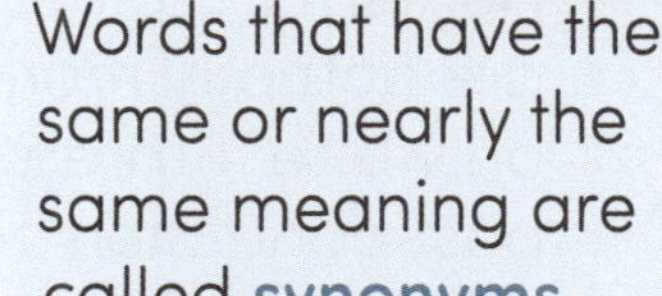

3 Find words in the word search that are synonyms for the words in the box.

X	S	Z	H	J	Q	G	U
Q	H	B	V	U	N	V	N
B	I	G	R	I	R	W	H
E	P	K	R	O	V	T	A
N	E	A	R	X	O	Y	P
T	L	V	Z	K	T	M	P
B	A	N	D	I	T	N	Y
C	O	R	R	E	C	T	X

boat
brush
circle
close
crooked
large
outlaw
injure
right
sad

Try it out!

Use a dictionary to help you find **synonyms** for these words. Write your answers on a separate piece of paper.

- fear
- create
- mimic
- bulky
- hideous

It's all about spiders!

Spiders and their close relatives, the scorpions, are called *arachnids*. To some people, spiders can be terrifying creatures. This fear of spiders is called *arachnophobia* (say **uh-rack-nuh-foh-bee-uh**). Let's look at some spiders to see if they deserve their reputation.

Huntsman spiders, although big and hairy, are generally harmless. They are actually more frightened of you than you need to be of them. They will only bite if threatened, preferring to run away. Huntsman spiders are good pest controllers to have around the house as they eat flies, mosquitoes and other nuisance pests.

Not so harmless are the male Sydney funnel-web spider and the female redback spider. Both of these spiders are highly venomous and they are the only Australian spiders known to have caused deaths.

There is no scientific evidence to support the myth that the venom of the daddy-long-legs spider is the most toxic of all spiders. The daddy-long-legs spider's fangs are tiny and are not capable of penetrating human skin.

So, as long as we take sensible precautions, such as shaking out footwear and clothing before putting them on, there really is no need to fear our eight-legged friends.

OXFORD UNIVERSITY PRESS

Writers use paragraphs to organise information. Paragraphs usually start with a topic sentence to introduce the main point being made in the paragraph. The sentences that follow usually provide us with further details about the topic sentence.

1 Read the report about spiders. There are five paragraphs. Write *first*, *second*, *third*, *fourth* or *last* to say which paragraphs match these descriptions.

a I am a paragraph about a spider myth. ____________________

b I am a paragraph about venomous spiders in Australia. ____________________

c I am a paragraph about huntsman spiders. ____________________

d I am the concluding paragraph. ____________________

e I am the introductory paragraph that classifies spiders. ____________________

2 Copy the topic sentence from the introductory paragraph that classifies spiders.

____

____

____

3 Write your own paragraph in which the main idea is about sharks or snakes and the starting topic is about the fear of these creatures.

____

____

____

____

____

Try it out!

Information reports such as this one about spiders often include technical language or scientific terms. Read the report again and write any words you think are scientific words that could be used about spiders.

____

____

Rain

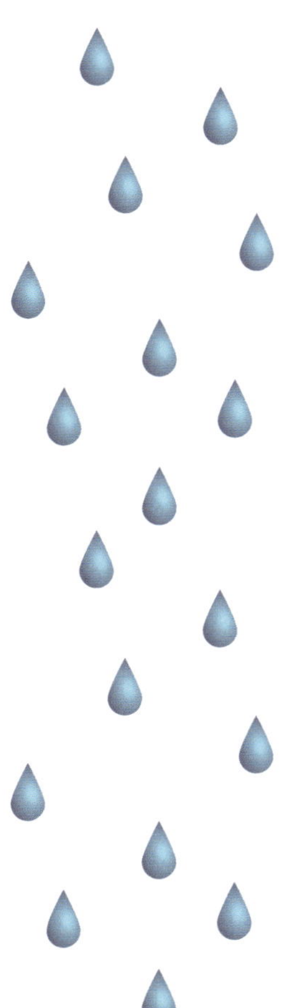

It's good to lie in bed at night
And hear the sweeping rain
Go patter patter on the roof
And knock against the pane.

It croaks and gurgles down the spout,
And swishes through the leaves,
And makes the curly creeper drip
That twines about the eaves.

All snug and warm in blankets soft
I hear a windy song
Like curlews in the lonely bush
That wail the whole night long.

L. H. Allen

Poets often use rhythm, alliteration and onomatopoeia to make their poems entertaining and easy to read.

Rhythm is the regular beat that makes the poem easy to read.

Alliteration is a group of words that begin with the same letter or sound. For example: *six silly sausages*

Onomatopoeia (say *on-oh-mat-uh-pee-uh*) is when words sound like the thing they are describing. For example: *Shush! Sizzle! Crack!*

1 Read "Rain". The writer has used onomatopoeia to show the reader the sounds he thinks rain makes. On the line below, write the onomatopoeic words the poet has used to describe rain.

____

2 Circle the examples of onomatopoeia used in these sentences.

a All night long the leaking tap went drip, drip drip.

b "Achoo!" sneezed Bardo, who had caught a cold.

c When Jirra poured milk onto his cereal, it crackled and crunched.

d All we could see was the flutter of butterfly wings.

3 Tick the sentence below that shows the best example of alliteration.

a Patter patter on the roof.

b Patter patter on the pane.

c Snug and warm in blankets soft.

4 Use onomatopoeia and the rhythm and rhyme of this poem to complete the final line in your own words.

Here comes trotting Dobbin

with old Harry up on top,

Here he comes a'cantering

____

Try it out!

The poem describes wailing curlews. What do you think a curlew might be?

____

Aaron

Hi, my name is Aaron.

I live in Yirrkala, which is in Arnhem Land, in the Northern Territory of Australia.

Aboriginal people have lived in Yirrkala for a very long time.

Where I live is tropical, which means it is warm all year round. That means that I can spend lots of time outside.

Living in a tropical place also means that, during the wet season, there might be cyclones. My school has been specially built to withstand a cyclone.

Many of the lessons at my school are taught outside. We learn practical things, such as how to fish and hunt.

I like the bush, and when I grow up I want to be a ranger like my dad. That way, I can teach other people about the bush.

1 Find words in the text “Aaron” that are antonyms for these words.

a cool ______________________ b dry ______________________

c short ______________________ d inside ______________________

2 Draw lines from the words in Box A to their synonyms in Box B.

A	B
live	instruct
many	hot
like	reside
tropical	enjoy
teach	lots

3 Use words from the box to complete these lines of alliteration.

fish butter rugged saucepan

a Seven savoury sausages sizzling in a ______________________ .

b Forty funny flying ______________________ with five fins each.

c Bobbi Barker’s baking bread to spread a bit of ______________________ on.

d Round and round the ______________________ rock the ragged rascal ran.

Try it out!

Can you add **onomatopoeic** words of your own to these pictures?

______________________ ______________________ ______________________

Topic 3: Test your grammar

Text cohesion and language devices

1. Shade the bubble next to the **antonym** (opposite) of the word **under**.
   - ○ inside ○ over ○ up ○ below

2. Shade the bubble next to the **antonym** (opposite) of the word **wide**.
   - ○ broad ○ heavy ○ narrow ○ thick

3. Shade the bubble next to the **antonym** (opposite) of the word **beautiful**.
   - ○ ugly ○ nice ○ attractive ○ handsome

4. Shade the bubble next to the **antonym** of the word **visible**.
   - ○ unvisible ○ imvisible ○ invisible ○ disvisible

5. Shade the bubble next to the **prefix** that can be added to **honest** to make it an opposite.
   - ○ un ○ mis ○ in ○ dis

6. Shade the bubble next to the **prefix** that can be added to **behave** to make it an opposite.
   - ○ un ○ mis ○ in ○ dis

7. Shade the bubble next to the **synonym** for **messy**.
   - ○ neat ○ untidy ○ lovely ○ new

8. Shade the bubble next to the **synonym** for **old**.
   - ○ new ○ clear ○ modern ○ ancient

9. Shade the bubble next to the **synonym** for **cries**.
   - ○ sweeps ○ weeps ○ sweets ○ peeps

10 Read this paragraph.

Syno Nym, the acrobat, entered the arena. The crowd clapped and Syno began his act. He stretched and bent then ran, jumped and soared. He landed cleanly on his feet and bowed to the audience.

Now shade the bubble next to the **topic sentence** from the above paragraph.

- ◯ Syno Nym, the acrobat, entered the arena.
- ◯ The crowd clapped and Syno began his act.
- ◯ He stretched and bent, then ran, jumped and soared.
- ◯ He landed cleanly on his feet and bowed to the audience.

11 Shade the bubble next to the example of **onomatopoeia**.

◯ clear ◯ water ◯ splash ◯ surf

12 Shade the bubble next to the example of **alliteration**.

- ◯ pop! bang! crash!
- ◯ on the road
- ◯ one, two, three
- ◯ five fine fellows

How am I doing?

Colour the boxes if you understand.

Antonyms are opposites. ☐

Synonyms are words that mean the same or nearly the same. ☐

Paragraphs are used to organise information. ☐

A topic sentence introduces the main point of a paragraph. ☐

Rhythm, alliteration and onomatopoeia can be used to make text, especially poetry, more entertaining. ☐

Topic 4: Sentences

Learning intentions

We are learning to write simple sentences and how we combine them to make compound sentences.

We are learning to identify the subject and verb in a simple sentence.

Unit 4.1 Simple sentences

Where's Dad?

A simple sentence is a group of words that make sense.
On their own, the following groups do not make sense:
is sitting *the bird* *on the branch*
If we reorder the groups and put them together, they make sense.
The bird is sitting on the branch. OR *On the branch the bird is sitting.*
OR *Sitting on the branch is the bird.*
All of these groups of words make sense. They are simple sentences.

A simple sentence has only one verb or verb group. For example: **The bird is sitting on the branch.**

1 Add your own words to make simple sentences.

a On the weekend ______________________ .

b The dog ran out of ______________________ .

c ______________________ into the swimming pool.

2 Join the sentence parts from each box so that you make four simple sentences about the picture opposite.

Who or what?

Dad Galoot ... The kookaburra ... Zip ...
Zac ... Zig and Zed ... Zeke ... Mum Galoot ...

Is doing what?

... is resting ...	... are fighting ...
... is sleeping ...	... is calling ...
... is laughing ...	... is perched ...
... is looking ...	... is aiming ...
... is playing ...	... is running ...

When? Where? How? Why?

... under the gum tree.	... with Zeke.
... around the tree.	... at Zip.
... for Dad Galoot.	... on a branch.
... at a can.	... from the porch.
... with each other.	... after breakfast.

____

____

____

____

Try it out!

On a piece of paper, unjumble these words to write one sentence.

on farm the live Galoots The a in country

Zoot Galoot at the Olympics

Zoot Galoot is at the Olympic Games. He has entered many events.

Zoot jumps very high. No one cheers.

Zoot scores all the goals. There is no cheering.

Zoot throws the shot-put. He sets a new record.

Zoot wins the race. He is the only runner.

Perhaps Zoot should have gone INSIDE the Olympic Stadium for his events.

Coordinating conjunctions (*and*, *but*, *so* and *or*) can be used to join simple sentences together to form longer, compound sentences.

For example: *The goblin was small* ***and*** *he was very strong.*

Akmed tried hard ***but*** *he lost the game.*

The plant died ***so*** *we put it into the compost bin.*

Compound sentences have two verbs or verb groups. For example: **The goblin was small, but he was strong.**

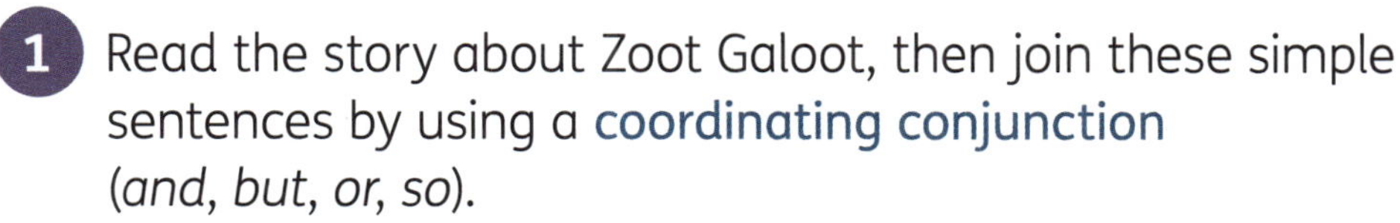

1 Read the story about Zoot Galoot, then join these simple sentences by using a coordinating conjunction (*and*, *but*, *or*, *so*).

a Zoot jumps very high. No one cheers.

____

b Zoot is the only runner. He wins the race.

____

c Zoot throws the shot-put. He sets a new record.

____

d Zoot scores lots of goals. There is no cheering.

____

2 Rewrite these sentences as compound sentences by joining them with *and*, *but*, *or* or *so*.

a It was raining. We couldn't go outside.

____

b We watered the seedlings often. They grew into pretty flowers.

____

c I would write it down. I don't have a pencil.

____

3 Circle the coordinating conjunctions in question 2 above.

Try it out!

Complete these **sentences** in your own words.

a I ran out of the room **and** ______________________________.

b ______________________________ **but** I didn't go.

c We arrived at the zoo early **so** ______________________________.

The Ogs' birthday party

We can change simple sentences into longer, more interesting sentences by:

- adding phrases
- using conjunctions
- adding adjectives and adverbs.

For example: *Og O is blowing out candles.* This simple sentence could become ...
Og O is on the table blowing out three candles on a huge birthday cake.

1 Use the picture of the Ogs' birthday party to help you make longer, more interesting sentences below.

a Og G has a frying pan.

____

b Og D is climbing a ladder.

____

c Og U is in a car.

____

d Og T has a balloon.

____

e There is a paddling pool.

____

2 Add a phrase to write a longer, more interesting sentence below.

The Ogs are having a birthday party.

____

____

____

Try it out!

On a piece of paper, write three of your own **longer, more interesting sentences** about the picture – one using a phrase (or phrases), one using a coordinating conjunction (**and**, **but**, **or, so**) and one using at least one adjective and one adverb.

For example: *Og V is happily pushing the blue car.*

Why the honeybee stings

A tale from Ancient Greece

The honeybee was unhappy. People were stealing her honey. The honeybee thought that all of the honey should be hers. She did not want to share any honey.

The honeybee went to Zeus, who was the chief god. She asked Zeus to give her the power to sting anyone who came near her hive. Zeus granted the honeybee's wish.

However, he was angry that the honeybee would be so mean. Zeus decided to teach her a lesson. He cast a spell that made the honeybee lose her sting when she used it on anyone.

Of course, today we know that honeybees do not only lose their stings when they use them. They also lose their lives.

Every simple sentence has a subject telling who or what the sentence is about.
Every simple sentence also has a verb. The subject and verb must agree. For example:

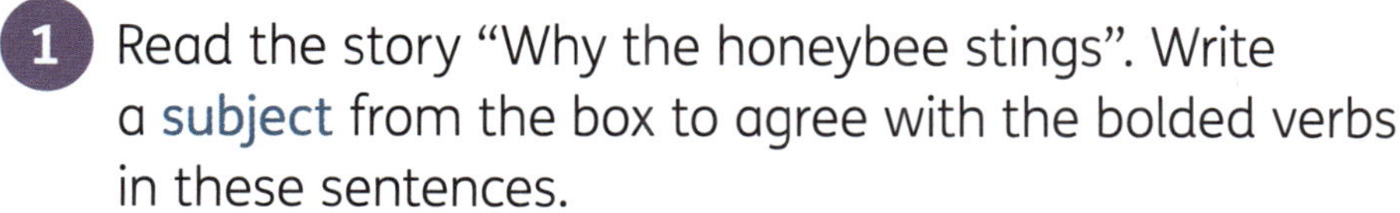

✓ *The honeybee is in the hive.* ✗ *The honeybee are in the hive.*

The second sentence is incorrect. It should be: *The honeybees are in the hive.*

A **simple sentence** has one main idea or **main clause**. It always has a subject and a verb or verb group.

1 Read the story "Why the honeybee stings". Write a subject from the box to agree with the bolded verbs in these sentences.

a ______________ **was** unhappy.

b ______________ **were stealing** honey.

c ______________ **would not share** her honey.

d ______________ **grants** the honeybee's wish.

e ______________ **have** striped bodies.

f ______________ **was** angry with the honeybee.

g ______________ **was** very mean.

h ______________ **know** all about honeybees now.

i ______________ **have** a sting on their tail.

Honeybees
The honeybee
Zeus
We
People

2 Circle the verb that agrees correctly with the subject in each of the sentences below.

a The monster **is** / **are** scary.

b Humpty Dumpty **was** / **were** on the wall.

c The honeybee **sting** / **stings**.

d Dogs **bark** / **barks**.

e I **like** / **likes** fish.

f We **has** / **have** a new teacher.

g The ship **is** / **are** at the port.

h They **is** / **are** upset.

3 Underline the subject in these sentences.

a Tractors pull heavy logs.

b Dad made a billycart for the children.

c Giraffes have long necks.

d The ship sank quickly.

Try it out!

Add your own **subject** to finish these sentences.

a ______________ was sitting at the bus stop waiting patiently.

b ______________ barked when the stranger came into the garden.

Common sense

(A story from Africa)

Anansi the spider thought of a good idea. He would gather up all the common sense in the world. That would make Anansi very powerful and all the animals would need to come to him for advice.

Anansi went about collecting common sense. He put all of it into an empty gourd (a large fruit shell). Anansi decided to hide his gourd at the top of a very tall tree. He tied one end of a rope around the neck of the gourd. He tied the other end around his neck so the huge gourd hung in front of him.

Anansi tried to climb the tree but the gourd was in his way. He could not stretch his arms and legs around the tree's trunk.

Anansi heard some laughter. He looked around and saw Monkey.

"You are a silly fellow," said Monkey. "If you had any common sense you would hang that gourd on your back so you can climb the tree."

Anansi was furious because he realised that Monkey still had some common sense. He smashed the gourd against the tree and common sense scattered everywhere. It was carried all around the world by the wind. That is why today everybody has a little common sense.

1 Complete these simple sentences from the story "Common sense".

a ______________________________ of a good idea.

b Anansi went about collecting ______________________________.

c ______________________________ some laughter.

Do you remember? **Coordinating conjunctions** can be used to join simple sentences together to make more interesting, longer sentences.

2 Circle the coordinating conjunctions in these sentences from the story of Anansi.

a He smashed the gourd against the tree and common sense scattered everywhere.

b Anansi tried to climb the tree but the gourd was in his way.

c He tied the other end around his neck so the huge gourd hung in front of him.

3 Circle the verb that agrees correctly with the subject in each of the sentences below.

a Common sense **was** / **were** scattered everywhere.

b "You **is** / **are** a silly fellow," said Monkey.

c That is why today everybody **have** / **has** a little common sense.

Try it out!

Can you improve these sentences by joining them with one of these **coordinating conjunctions**?

and but so

a Anansi heard some laughter. He looked around.

____

b Anansi stretched out his legs. They would not fit around the tree's trunk.

____

c He smashed the gourd against the tree. Common sense scattered everywhere.

____

Topic 4: Test your grammar

Sentences

1 Shade the bubble next to the simple sentence.

- ◯ near the house
- ◯ at sunset
- ◯ We climbed the hill.
- ◯ The weary walkers crossed the stream so they could reach the camp.

2 Shade the bubble next to the group of words that could be added to the following sentence beginning to form a simple sentence.

The girl [ ]

◯ shut the window. ◯ on the bridge ◯ happy ◯ quickly

3 Shade the bubble next to the group of words that could be added to the following sentence ending to form a simple sentence.

[ ] *at the clown.*

◯ on fire ◯ The circus ◯ We laughed ◯ was funny

4 Shade the bubble next to the verb that completes this sentence.

The children [ ] *playing in the park.*

◯ is ◯ am ◯ are ◯ was

5 Shade the bubble next to the verb that completes this sentence.

Kangaroos [ ] *in Australia.*

◯ live ◯ lived ◯ lives ◯ living

6 Shade the bubble next to the verb that completes this sentence.

We [ ] *expecting the tram to arrive at 9 o'clock.*

◯ is ◯ were ◯ was ◯ am

7 Shade the bubble next to the coordinating conjunction that best completes this sentence.

The cat was tired [ ] *it curled up and went to sleep.*

○ and ○ but ○ so ○ or

8 Shade the bubble next to the coordinating conjunction that best completes this sentence.

I made a cheese sandwich [ ] *I ate it for my lunch.*

○ and ○ but ○ so ○ or

9 Shade the bubble next to the coordinating conjunction that best completes this sentence.

My grandpa is very old [ ] *he is still fit and strong.*

○ and ○ but ○ so ○ or

10 Shade the bubble next to the sentence that is **not** a simple sentence.

○ Ducks like bread.
○ Skye is tall and she has dark hair.
○ The dog tried to steal the meat.
○ The sharp-eyed eagle soared majestically into the sky.

11 Rewrite this simple sentence as a longer, more interesting sentence.

Frogs croak.

____

How am I doing?

Colour the boxes if you understand.

Sentences must make sense. ☐

A simple sentence has one main idea or main clause and one verb or verb group. ☐

A compound sentence has two verbs or verb groups. ☐

Coordinating conjunctions can be used to join simple sentences to make longer, more interesting sentences. ☐

The subject and the verb of a sentence must agree. ☐

Topic 5: Sentences and punctuation

Learning intention

We are learning to use correct punctuation when writing sentences for different purposes, for example, using a capital letter at the start of a sentence or for proper nouns; using question marks for questions and exclamation marks for exclamations; and using commas and apostrophes.

Unit 5.1 Capital letters

Zoot Galoot – Space ace!

Zoot Galoot, ace space pilot, relaxes in his comfy chair and flips a control button.

A Gorgon spacefighter from the Medusa Galaxy is heading straight at Zoot. He dives for cover.

Suddenly, a terrifying monster appears. It moves towards Zoot. The space ace covers his eyes.

A train appears from nowhere and charges at Zoot. He hides behind his comfy chair.

A great ball of fire hurtles towards Zoot. It is a comet. In a few seconds, Zoot will be smashed into a million pieces. There is nowhere left for Zoot to hide.

The comet comes **closer,**

closer,

closer...

So Zoot switches off the TV and goes outside to play.

Capital letters are used at the beginning of sentences.
For example: *The spaceship crashed in the paddock.*

Use capital letters: at the beginning of a sentence, for proper nouns, for the word *I*.

1 Read the story, then write the following sentences using the correct punctuation.

a he is hiding behind his chair.

____

b a spacefighter is heading straight at him.

____

c in a few seconds, Zoot will be smashed into a million pieces.

____

d the fireball moves towards Zoot.

____

Capital letters are used for special names (proper nouns) of people, places and things.

2 Write these proper nouns using the correct punctuation.

a roald dahl ______________ **b** zoot galoot ______________

c sunday ______________ **d** new south wales ______________

e january ______________ **f** hume freeway ______________

The word *I* is always written with a capital letter.

3 Rewrite the following sentences using the correct punctuation.

a in the hall, i saw mr cheng's coat and new umbrella.

____

b ben, ari and i travelled together to sydney.

____

c when i saw elvis rasheed in knight street, i called out to him and waved.

____

____

Try it out!

On a piece of paper, use the correct **punctuation** to write the names of:

- three members of your family
- an alien spaceship
- a book you have enjoyed reading
- five days of the week.

The heartbeat of the land (Part 1)

This is a story about Cathy Freeman. **See Part 2 on page 80.**

Cathy ran barefoot every day across the great ancient land, as her people had done for sixty thousand years before.

Each morning, Cathy chased the wungar high into the sky. Every night she chased it back to bed again.

She was as swift as the wind and as fast as the birds because her ancestors had decided it from long ago. And when she ran she could hear the heartbeat of the land. Ba boom Ba boom Ba boom

One hot dusty day, the heartbeat grew quiet. Cathy listened closely. The rocks cried out, the sky groaned and the mountains wailed. "Why are you crying?", she asked.

"The land is sick," they said. "The jalun is getting too hot. The juku wubal are disappearing and the wawubaja are drying up."

Cathy's heart began to beat fast. She knew what she had to do.

She quickly filled her pockets with handfuls of seeds and off she ran.

She ran as fast as she could to the north. She ran as fast as she could to the south.

She chased the wungar from the east to the west and back again, spreading seeds as she went.

Cathy Freeman with Coral Vass

wungar = sun jalun = ocean juku wubal = trees wawubaja = rivers

Go to Unit 5.7 to read the end of this story.

Statements are sentences that state facts, give opinions or tell information of some sort.
A statement always begins with a capital letter and ends with a full stop.
For example: *The animals, birds and plants knew only night.*

1 Unjumble these words to write statements from the story.

a every day great ancient land. Cathy ran barefoot across the

____

b quiet. heartbeat grew One hot dusty day, the

____

c and off she ran. with handfuls of seeds She quickly filled her pockets

____

d chased the wungar high Each morning, into the sky. Cathy

____

2 Write statements of your own using these beginnings.

a Every night ________________________________.

b One hot dusty day, ________________________________.

c And when she ran ________________________________.

3 Rewrite these statements, adding capital letters and full stops where they belong.

a the sky groaned and the mountains wailed

____

b she ran as fast as she could

____

4 Write statements of your own using these endings.

a ________________________________ my next birthday.

b ________________________________ in the forest.

Try it out!

On a piece of paper, write five **statements** that tell us something about you. Make sure that not all of your statements begin with **I** and that your statements are complete sentences.

Don't ask me!

Mum, why is the
sky so blue?

Don't ask me
now, for I've
work here to do.

Uncle Rob, why
is the water in
my bath so wet?

Don't ask me
that, for I've
shopping to get.

Sister Sue, why
does the Sun chase
after the Moon?

I'll answer that
question on the
thirty-first of June.

Why is that so,
Dad? Won't you
say more?

Tell me Dad, why
does time fly when
we're having fun?

Now, too many
questions are not
good for you, Son.

Save up your
questions. What do
you think school is for?

When we want an answer to something, we ask a question. A question ends with a question mark (?). Some words that can ask questions are: *How? What? Where? When? Why?*

1 Tick the sentences below that ask questions.

- **a** Why is the sky so blue? ☐
- **b** I've shopping to get. ☐
- **c** When does time fly? ☐
- **d** What do you think school is for? ☐
- **e** Save up your questions, Son. ☐
- **f** Come here, Son! ☐
- **g** Is the Sun chasing the Moon? ☐
- **h** Are you going to answer my questions? ☐

2 Write questions that you think might have been asked to get the following answers.

a ______________________________ ? My name is Marie.

b ______________________________ ? I am nine years old.

c ______________________________ ? My new jumper is red.

d ______________________________ ? It is nearly three o'clock.

e ______________________________ ? He told us to put our books away.

f ______________________________ ?

On Saturday, I am going shopping for a birthday present.

g ______________________________ ?

If the ball goes through the ring, your team scores two points.

3 Write your own question in the speech bubble of this cartoon.

Try it out!

Questioning words are often used at the beginning of **questions**.
For example: **What** ? **How** ?
How many questioning words can you write?

Pardon me!

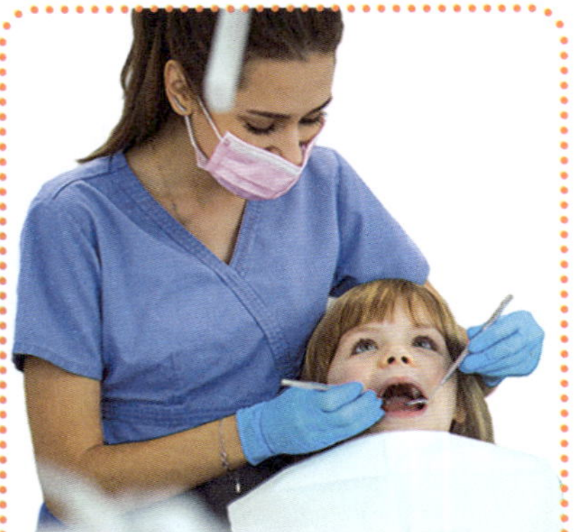

All aboard!

Look out!

Kick it to me!

Go team!

Oh, my goodness!
Midnight already!

Open wide!

Help! The giant's
after me!

Great work!

Boo!

OXFORD UNIVERSITY PRESS

Some sentences can be very short.

Some short sentences are called exclamations.

We use an exclamation when something is said suddenly, loudly and with feeling (fright, anger or pleasure).

An exclamation begins with a capital letter and ends with an exclamation mark (**!**).

For example: *Get out now! Don't do that!*

1 In "Pardon me!", you can see nine exclamations and nine characters.

Write the best exclamation for each character in the spaces below.

a " ______________________________ " yelled the builder.

b " ______________________________ " cheered the sports fan.

c " ______________________________ " called the railway announcer.

d " ______________________________ " said the monster.

e " ______________________________ " called the football player.

f " ______________________________ " said the teacher.

g " ______________________________ " said the dentist.

h " ______________________________ " cried Jack.

i " ______________________________ " shrieked Cinderella.

2 Write an exclamation for the cartoon below. Don't forget your exclamation mark!

Try it out!

Write an **exclamation** that you might make:

- on your birthday. ______________________________
- when your team scores the winning goal. ______________________________
- when you are warning someone. ______________________________

What's in Granny Og's shopping bag?

a long, thin, healthy loaf of bread

a packet of chewy, juicy Fruit Joobs

a bunch of large, ripe, yellow bananas, oranges, pears, grapes and apples

hard, holey cheese

potatoes, carrots, an eggplant, celery and a huge, round pumpkin

soft, squishy cheese

half a dozen delicious, farm-fresh, free-range eggs

and a large, gaping hole

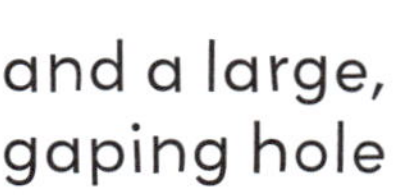

Commas can be used to separate nouns in a list. For example: *horses, cows, ducks, pigs and sheep*
Commas can be used to separate adjectives in a list. For example: *the fast, new, red car*

1 Read "What's in Granny Og's shopping bag?" and then add commas where you think they belong in these sentences.

- **a** Granny Og bought apples oranges pears and grapes at the OgMart.
- **b** There was a large gaping hole in the bottom of her shopping bag.
- **c** The long thin loaf of bread was sticking out of the bag.
- **d** The potatoes carrots eggplant and celery fell out of Granny Og's shopping bag.

Don't use a comma at the end of a list if the word **and** has been used. Don't use a comma to separate an adjective immediately before a noun.

2 **a** The commas in this sentence are in the wrong places. Rewrite the sentence with the commas where they belong.

Granny bought some soft squishy, cheese and some potatoes carrots, and pumpkin.

____

____

____

____

b What would you buy for dinner tonight? Write a sentence, listing all the food items you would buy.

____

____

____

Try it out!

On a piece of paper, write three sentences listing your four favourite colours, six animals you might see at the zoo and five sports or games you like to watch or play. Don't forget to use **commas** to separate the things in your lists. Use these beginnings for your sentences.

- My favourite colours are ...
- At the zoo I might see ...
- I like to watch or play ...

Unit 5.6 Apostrophes of contraction and possession

My puppy

It's funny
my puppy
knows just how I feel.
When I'm happy
he's yappy
and squirms like
an eel.

When I'm grumpy
he's slumpy
and stays at my heel.
It's funny
my puppy
knows such a
great deal.

Aileen Fisher

Mitch and Titch

Mitch went into a warm café
to escape the biting blizzard
and sitting upon his shoulder
there appeared to be a lizard.
"I think I'll have a tea," said Mitch
and, with a nod to the reptile, said,
"Titch here will have an orange juice
then I'll take him home to bed."
The waiter scratched her head
and asked,
"Why do you call him Titch?"
"Now isn't that plainly obvious?
Cause he's my newt!" said Mitch.

AjW

Some words can be made shorter by leaving out letters.

When we are speaking informally with family or friends, words are often shortened by taking out letters. These shortened words are called contractions. We replace the letters with a mark like this **’**. This mark is called an apostrophe.

For example: *I’m = I am* *we’ll = we will* *she’d = she would or she had* *can’t = cannot*
An apostrophe can also be used to show that something belongs to someone.

1 Write the contractions from the poems next to their partners below.

it’s he’s I’ll I’m isn’t don’t

a I will ______ **b** it is ______

c he is ______ **d** I am ______

e is not ______ **f** do not ______

An apostrophe looks a little like a flying comma.
An apostrophe of contraction shows us that letters have been left out.
An apostrophe of possession shows us who owns something or is connected to someone.

2 Shorten these words by writing an apostrophe where the missing letters should go.
For example: *I have = I’ve* (The apostrophe takes the place of *h* and *a*.)

a I am = ______ **b** cannot = ______

c I will = ______ **d** did not = ______

3 Rewrite the sentences, adding an apostrophe and **s** (’s) to show who owns something.

a The hat of Mitch. ______

b The notepad of the waiter. ______

4 Imagine Mitch has more than one newt named Titch. Rewrite the sentences to show that the newts own something, adding an apostrophe (’) correctly.

a The home of the newts.

______

b The bed of the newts.

______

Try it out!

On a piece of paper, write three sentences using **apostrophes** to show possession (both singular and plural) and include some **contractions**.
For example: *The local park’s playground isn’t big.*

The heartbeat of the land (Part 2)

This a story about Cathy Freeman. Go to Unit 5.2 to read the start of the story.

Soon people gathered to watch. They were puzzled. "What are you doing?", they asked. "The land is sick. It needs our help," said Cathy. "Take these seeds and plant as many as you can. They will grow, clean the air and save our land."

At first, the people were too busy to listen. They were too distracted to stop, and too occupied to help. But little by little, some people began to hear the cry of the land. They took the seeds and planted them near the rivers, over the plains and even in the towns and cities.

When the last seeds were planted, the rocks beamed, the sky breathed and the mountains echoed with joy. Cathy listened again and smiled ... Ba boom Ba boom Ba boom

Cathy ran barefoot every day across the great ancient land. Each morning, Cathy chased the wungar high into the sky. Every night she chased it back to bed again. And when she ran, she always heard the heartbeat of the land.

Cathy Freeman with Coral Vass

wungar = Sun

1. After each sentence write *S* if it is a statement, write *Q* if it is a question and write *E* if it is an exclamation.

   a. Soon people gathered to watch. ____________________

   b. "What are you doing?" ____________________

   c. They planted the seeds near the rivers. ____________________

   d. The mountains echoed with joy! ____________________

2. Write the commas where they correctly belong in these sentences.

   a. They will grow clean the air and save our land.

   b. Each morning Cathy chased the wungar high into the sky.

   c. When the last seeds were planted the rocks beamed the sky breathed and the mountains echoed with joy.

3. Rewrite these sentences so that the contraction is written in full.

   For example: You'd better be quiet when filling your billycan.

   You had better be quiet when filling your billy can.

   a. They'll grow and clean the air. ____________________

   b. It's well known that trees clean the air. ____________________

   c. If you listen carefully, you'll hear the heartbeat of the land.

   d. She'll keep running every morning and every night.

Try it out!

In your own words, explain why the people in the story were too busy to listen.

____

Why do you think Cathy smiles at the end of the story?

____

Topic 5: Test your grammar

Sentences and punctuation

1 Shade the bubble next to the sentence that has the correct **punctuation**.

- ◯ sam and rupert were walking up jackson street when they saw molly
- ◯ Sam and rupert were walking up jackson street when they saw molly.
- ◯ Sam and Rupert were walking up Jackson Street when they saw Molly.
- ◯ Sam and rupert were walking up Jackson street when they saw molly.

2 Shade the bubble with the word that should begin with a **capital letter**.

◯ school ◯ saturday ◯ happy ◯ today

3 Shade the bubble next to the sentence that has the correct **punctuation**.

- ◯ on friday i went to the cinema and watched *born to ride*
- ◯ On Friday i went to the cinema and watched *Born to Ride*.
- ◯ On Friday I Went to the Cinema and Watched *Born to Ride*.
- ◯ On Friday I went to the cinema and watched *Born to Ride*.

4 Shade the bubble next to the **punctuation** mark that is missing from this sentence.

Did you see how big the moon was last night

◯ . ◯ ? ◯ ! ◯ ,

5 Shade the bubble next to the **punctuation** mark that is missing from this sentence.

The flowers in the garden were all in bloom

◯ . ◯ ? ◯ ! ◯ ,

6 Shade the bubble next to the **punctuation** mark that is missing from this sentence.

Watch out Lockie

◯ . ◯ ? ◯ ! ◯ ,

OXFORD UNIVERSITY PRESS

7 Shade the bubble next to the sentence that has the correct **punctuation**.

- ◯ At the aquarium we saw angelfish, jellyfish, sharks and an octopus.
- ◯ At the aquarium we saw angelfish, jellyfish, sharks, and, an octopus.
- ◯ At the aquarium, we saw angelfish, jellyfish, sharks, and an octopus.
- ◯ At the aquarium we saw angelfish jellyfish sharks and an octopus,

8 Shade the bubble next to the sentence that has the correct **punctuation**.

- ◯ Sitting on a large red toadstool was a strange little old elf.
- ◯ Sitting, on a large red toadstool, was a strange little old elf.
- ◯ Sitting on a large, red, toadstool, was a strange, little, old elf.
- ◯ Sitting on a large, red toadstool was a strange, little, old elf.

9 Shade the bubble next to the word with the **apostrophe** in the correct place.

◯ could'nt ◯ coul'dnt ◯ couldn't ◯ couldnt'

10 Shade the bubble next to the **contraction** for **she will**.

◯ shell ◯ shel'l
◯ sh'ell ◯ she'll

How am I doing?

Colour the boxes if you understand.

- Capital letters begin sentences. ☐
- Capital letters begin proper nouns. ☐
- **I** is always written as a capital letter. ☐
- Statements end with full stops. ☐
- Questions end with question marks. ☐
- Exclamations end with exclamation marks. ☐
- Commas can be used to separate nouns or adjectives in a list. ☐
- An apostrophe of contraction shows that a letter or letters have been left out. ☐

Topic 6: Using grammar

Learning intention

We are learning about informative, imaginative and persuasive texts and the type of language, punctuation and grammar we would find in them.

Unit 6.1 Using grammar in informative texts (information report)

Gangurrus, kangaroos

Fact file

The word *kangaroo* comes from the Aboriginal word *gangurru*. *Gangurru* is a word in the language of the Guugu Yimithirr people, whose traditional land is in Far North Queensland.

Kangaroos are one of Australia's most famous animals. All kangaroos are marsupials called macropods, meaning "large foot". A marsupial is a mammal that carries its baby in a pouch.

Kangaroos have powerful back legs to help them hop, and they use their strong tail to help them balance. Kangaroos can hop for long distances at a time.

Baby kangaroos are born all year round. Soon after birth, the baby kangaroo, called a joey, climbs into its mother's pouch. Joeys feed and grow in this pouch for nine months.

joey

pouch

large feet

powerful tail

Kangaroos are found in every state and territory in Australia. Their habitats range from warm, tropical rainforests and deserts to the colder climates of the southern states.

Kangaroos are herbivores. They eat plants such as grass and leaves.

Information reports are usually written in paragraphs, sometimes with a subheading for each one, to organise bundles of information. The first paragraph is used to introduce or classify the subject. The paragraphs that follow often start with a topic sentence to introduce the main idea of the paragraph.

1 Read "Gangurrus, kangaroos". Highlight the topic sentence at the start of each paragraph, then, using the subheadings below, label each paragraph in the report.

How kangaroos move | How they got their name | A famous marsupial

Baby kangaroos | What they eat | Where they live

Simple sentences are often used in information reports to state facts. For example: *Kangaroos are herbivores.*

Compound sentences, using coordinating conjunctions, are often used to compare details.

For example: *Kangaroos eat grass and leaves, but they also eat flowers, fruit and moss.*

2 Write your own simple sentence to share another fact you know about kangaroos.

____

3 Read the paragraph that describes how kangaroos move. Write the compound sentence in this paragraph, then circle the coordinating conjunction.

____

____

Information reports are usually written in the present tense, using doing verbs and relating verbs (being and having verbs).

4 Circle the correct present tense relating verb to complete each sentence below.

a Female kangaroos **has** / **have** pouches.

b A kangaroo **is** / **are** a powerful animal.

c There **is** / **are** different types of kangaroos.

d That kangaroo **has** / **have** a baby joey.

Try it out!

On a piece of paper, write your own **paragraph** to describe what a kangaroo looks like. Include at least two **adjectives**.

Big, bad Barnaby Batteram

Captain Barnaby Batteram **was** a big, bad, mean pirate with a scar on his face and a patch over his left eye. Together with his loyal crew, he **had been plundering** the seven seas for many, many years, stealing gold and jewels and burying the precious treasure in secret caves along rugged cliffs and deserted beaches.

However, not only **was** Captain Barnaby big and bad and mean, he also **had** a very bad memory. On some days, Barmy, as his crew **called** him, **forgot** over which eye he usually **wore** his patch. On these days, the crew just **smiled** and **continued** "shivering their timbers".

This is so embarrassing.

On other days, Barmy **forgot** how to make his prisoners walk the plank. His crew just **smiled** and **said**, "Oh well, me hearties" and **carried on swabbing** the decks.

Sometimes this fearsome but forgetful pirate **forgot** how close his ship **needed** to be for boarding the rich galleons he **wanted to plunder** and **rob**.

When this **happened**, Barmy's crew **pretended** they **didn't** know him. They just **looked** the other way, all embarrassed.

Unfortunately, the most worrying thing that Captain Barnaby Batteram often **forgot was** where he **had** buried the pirates' treasure chest. When this **happened**, his crew **gave** him a very severe look. Sometimes they **wouldn't** talk to Barmy for the rest of the day!

Follow me lads. Aaghhhh!

Imaginative narratives, such as the one about Captain Barnaby Batteram, start with an orientation paragraph. Phrases and adjectives are used to describe the characters and set the scene to tell us where and when this story has taken place.

1 Read the story of "Big, bad Barnaby Batteram". Write the adjectives the author has used in the orientation paragraph to introduce the characters and set the scene.

a *Main character, Captain Barnaby Batteram:* ______________________.

b *Other characters – his crew:* ______________________.

c *Where?* ______________ seas, ______________ caves, ______________ cliffs, ______________ beaches

d *When?* For ______________ years

2 Use a phrase to add details to these sentences.

a Captain Barmy wore a patch ______________________.

b He was a mean pirate with a scar ______________________.

In the second paragraph of the story, the main character has a problem. The author uses adjectives to show how the main character has changed.

3 Choose adjectives from the box to complete each noun group below – one noun group for a strong character, the other for a weak character.

big forgetful older fearsome mean little

a *Strong character:* a ______________________ pirate

b *Weak character:* a ______________________ man

4 Find an antonym from the story for each word below.

a small ______________ b good ______________

Try it out!

Look at the bold verbs in "Big, bad Barnaby Batteram". The author has written this story in the **past tense** to show that it has already happened. With a partner, take turns reading each paragraph as if it is happening now, in the **present tense**. Write three examples of **present tense verbs** you used.

______________ ______________ ______________

Homework – Good or bad?

Homework is bad! It is bad because it is a waste of time.

When children come home from school they are tired. They should be allowed to relax and play computer games, watch TV or play sport.

Children spend six hours a day, five days a week learning at school. Doing school work at home is not fair!

Of course we need to learn, but doing school work at home is not the only way to learn.

Ben E. (Year 3)

I love doing homework!

When I get home from school, I have a snack and a drink and then Mum and I sit down at my table and do my homework together. It is a great way for us to spend some time together. If I get stuck, Mum is there to help me out!

Once I finish my homework, I can go out to play or watch television.

I know that doing my homework will help me with my other school work, so I think homework is good.

Elly B. (Year 3)

Persuasive texts are used to convince readers of something. Persuasive texts often use exclamations to make a point or show strong feelings.

1 Read the two persuasive texts on the opposite page.

a Write the two exclamations Ben uses in his text.

____

____

b Write the two exclamations Elly uses in her text.

____

____

Persuasive texts or arguments are usually written in the present tense. They often use thinking and feeling verbs to give opinions and modal verbs to tell about the certainty of something happening.

2 Use verbs in the present tense to complete these argument statements.

a "When children come home from school they ____________________," said Ben.

b "Mum and I ____________________ time together," said Elly.

c "When I ____________________ my homework, I can go out to play," said Elly.

3 Circle the thinking and feeling verbs in these sentences.

a I love doing my homework.

b Ben considers homework to be a bad thing.

c We prefer to go out and play than do homework.

4 Find modal verbs on the opposite page to complete the sentences.

a Doing my homework ____________________ help me with my other school work.

b Children ____________________ be allowed to relax and play computer games.

Try it out!

Which of the two sentences below makes a stronger argument by including an **adverb**?

☐ I believe homework is good for you.

☐ I truly believe homework is good for you.

Topic 7: Extension and enrichment

Learning intention

We are learning to understand and correctly use speech marks (quotation marks) and prepositions; write homophones and homonyms; and use prefixes and suffixes to expand our vocabulary and make our writing interesting.

Unit 7.1 Quoted (direct) speech

Doctor! Doctor!

Doctor Brown!
Doctor Brown!
I keep thinking that
I'm a strawberry.

Dear me, Kevin.
You really are in a
jam, aren't you?

Doctor Black: What seems to be the trouble?
Maree: I swallowed a clock last week.
Doctor Black: My goodness, why didn't you come sooner?
Maree: I didn't want to alarm anybody.

Dr Yellow: Zoe, how did you get here so fast?
Zoe: Flu.

"Doctor, Doctor, you must help me," said Paul. "I can't remember anything."
"How long has this been going on?" asked Doctor Green.
"How long has what been going on?" said Paul.

Doctor Blue!
Doctor Blue!
I feel like a
pack of cards.

Just sit there,
Jenny, and I'll deal
with you later.

"Doctor Red, I've got beans growing out of my ears," cried Jan.
"Oh dear," said Doctor Red.
"How did that happen?"
"I've no idea," said Jan.
"I planted onions."

We can show that someone is speaking and we can show the words that are being spoken in a number of ways. Quoted (direct) speech refers to words that are actually spoken.

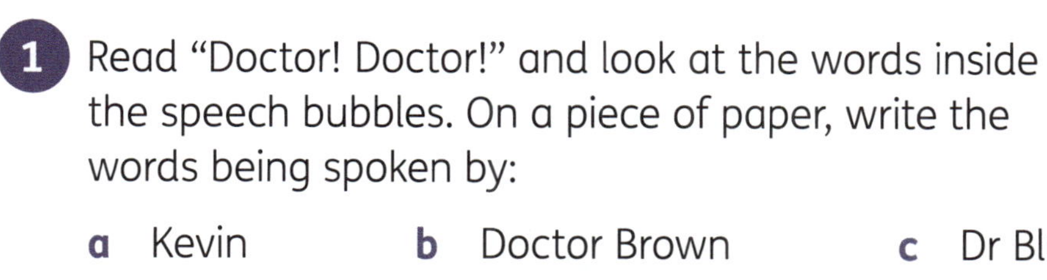

Quoted (direct) speech is sometimes written in a speech bubble or it can be written inside speech marks (quotation marks).

1 Read "Doctor! Doctor!" and look at the words inside the speech bubbles. On a piece of paper, write the words being spoken by:

a Kevin **b** Doctor Brown **c** Dr Blue

2 Another way to show spoken words is to write them in the form of a play, as shown in the conversation between Doctor Black and Maree on the opposite page.

Write some words spoken by:

a Dr Black: ____________________

b Maree: ____________________

c Doctor Yellow: ____________________

3 Another way to show spoken words in your writing is to use speech marks (quotation marks). For example: *"Help me!" yelled Rex*. What did Rex say? *Help me!*

Write some words spoken by:

a Paul: " ____________________ "

____

b Dr Green: " ____________________ "

c Jan: " ____________________ "

____

4 Use quoted (direct) speech to finish this famous conversation.

"Oh my, my, Grandma. What big eyes you have," said Little Red Riding Hood.

"All the better to see you with, my dear," said the Big Bad Wolf.

"Oh my, my, Grandma. What big ears you have," said Little Red Riding Hood.

" ____________________ ," said the Big Bad Wolf.

" ____________________ ," said Little Red Riding Hood.

____

Try it out!

On a piece of paper, write out a "Knock, knock" joke as if spoken by you and your best friend. Remember to show who is saying what.

The building Ogs

The word preposition means "placed in front of". Prepositions are usually placed *in front of* nouns and pronouns to form prepositional phrases. For example: *up the ladder, with her*

1 Look at the picture of "The building Ogs". Use prepositions from the box to form prepositional phrases telling where you will find each Og. Some prepositions may be used more than once.

a Og A is standing __________ a ladder.
b Og B is __________ the can of paint.
c Og D is leaning __________ the edge.
d Og F is __________ top of the roof.
e Og G will land __________ a sharp nail.
f Og H is sliding __________ the roof.
g Og J is __________ the water tank.
h Ogs L and N are carrying a plank __________ their shoulders.
i Og M is __________ the plank.
j Og O is walking __________ the door.
k Og P is __________ the wheelbarrow.
l Og S will be covered __________ sand.
m Og R is hanging __________ the roof.

off
in
down
on
under
by
from
above
over
with
through
behind

2 Write your own sentences using these prepositions.

a in __________

b off __________

c at __________

Try it out!

Use the picture on the opposite page and the following Ogs and **prepositions** to write your own sentences.

Og I = under __________

Og C = in __________

Og B = against __________

Hommy Nym juggles!

Homonyms are words that look and/or sound the same.
For example: *Wind the window out and let the wind in please.*
Most homonyms look different but sound the same. These homonyms are called homophones.
For example: *cheap* (not expensive), *cheep* (a bird's call)

1 Match the homophones in the box with the things that Hommy Nym juggles.

For example: *Hommy juggles a hoarse horse, a stake in a steak, etc.*

hoarse	tale	son	leek	leak	horse	tail
deer	steak	sun	dear	stake	pear	pair

Hommy juggles ______________________________

____

____

Words that sound the same but are spelled differently and have different meanings are called **homophones**.

2 Match the homophones in the box with their meanings.

week weak male mail ball bawl see sea steel steal one won

a a man or boy ______________
b look at ______________
c not strong ______________
d cry loudly ______________
e a single thing ______________
f seven days ______________
g a metal ______________
h salty water ______________
i letters and parcels ______________
j the past of *win* ______________
k take something that belongs to someone else ______________
l a round or egg-shaped bouncy thing ______________

3 Circle the correct homophone to match the picture.

flower/flour 
meet/meat 
sent/cent/scent 
poor/pour 
sell/cell 
creek/creak 

Try it out!

On a piece of paper, draw one of the following:

- a ewe chasing you
- a knight at night
- a hare with hair
- a doe eating dough
- a male delivering mail
- someone with a board who is bored.

Ridiculous rhymes

Careless Connie climbed a ladder
her aim to reach the top,
But Careless Connie was not careful –
she forgot to stop!

Ollie bought a magic kit
and practised for a year.
Now Ollie's finally mastered it
and made Ollie disappear.

"Please be helpful," said my dad
"and go outside to play."
"But Dad, we're in a submarine
on the bottom of the bay!"

AjW

A **prefix** comes at the beginning of a word. A **prefix** changes the meaning of a word.

1 Add one of the **prefixes** from the box to change the meanings of these words to opposites. The prefixes can be used more than once.

dis-
un-
im-
in-
mis-

a ________ fair

b ________ appear

c ________ lock

d ________ possible

e ________ visible

f ________ behave

g ________ respect

h ________ perfect

A **suffix** comes at the end of a word. A **suffix** also changes the meaning of a word.

2 Add the **suffixes** *-ful* and *-less* to write each of these words as **antonyms** (opposites).
For example: use = useful, useless

a care ____________________ ____________________

b rest ____________________ ____________________

c help ____________________ ____________________

d colour ____________________ ____________________

e power ____________________ ____________________

f doubt ____________________ ____________________

g harm ____________________ ____________________

h thank ____________________ ____________________

Try it out!

Add **prefixes** or change the **suffixes** of these words to make them opposites.

a possible ____________________ b obey ____________________

c merciful ____________________ d fearless ____________________

Who said that?

1. "Who's been eating my porridge?" said Papa Bear.

2. "I'll huff and I'll puff and I'll blow your house down!" shouted the Wolf.

3. "Why Grandma, what big eyes you have," said the little girl.

4. "Run, run as fast as you can. You can't catch me!" teased the tiny fellow.

5. "I had a terrible night's sleep," she moaned. "There was a lump in all those mattresses."

6. "Sorry, Prince," the beautiful girl gasped, "it's almost midnight and I have to leave right now!"

7. "Hey Jack!" called the seller. "Would you like to trade your cow for a few beans?"

8. "Mirror, Mirror on the wall, who is the fairest of them all?" asked the Queen.

1. Use the **direct speech** on the opposite page to help you answer these questions.

   a Who was talking to Jack? ______________________

   b Who asked a question about porridge? ______________________

   c Why did someone have a bad night's sleep? ______________________
   ____

   d Who is saying something threatening? ______________________

   e Who was the beautiful girl talking to? ______________________

2. Write the actual words spoken by these characters on the opposite page.

   a The Queen ______________________
   ____
   ____

   b The little girl ______________________
   ____
   ____

   c The seller ______________________
   ____
   ____

Try it out!

Write numbers to match these fairy tales with the **direct speech** on the opposite page.

- [ ] The Gingerbread Man
- [ ] Goldilocks and the Three Bears
- [ ] Jack and the Beanstalk
- [ ] The Three Little Pigs
- [ ] Little Red Riding Hood
- [ ] The Princess and the Pea
- [ ] Cinderella
- [ ] Snow White and the Seven Dwarfs

Topics 6 and 7: Test your grammar

Using grammar

1 Shade the bubble that shows the correct **direct speech** for the cartoon.

- ◯ What do bees do with their honey asked Mika. They cell it answered Trin.
- ◯ Mika asked what bees do with their honey and Trin said they cell it.
- ◯ "What do bees do with their honey?" asked Mika. "They cell it," answered Trin.
- ◯ What do bees do with their honey, "asked Mika?" They cell it, "answered Trin."

2 Shade the bubble that shows the **homophone** from the cartoon above.

◯ cell ◯ do ◯ honey ◯ with

3 Shade the bubble that shows the **preposition** in this **phrase**.

under the shady tree

◯ under ◯ the ◯ shady ◯ tree

4 Shade the bubble that shows a sentence with a **prepositional phrase**.

- ◯ "Look out!" he shouted.
- ◯ I like to eat cheese nibbles.
- ◯ He could clearly see a koala in the tree.
- ◯ The boy's name was Sayeed.

5 Shade the bubble that shows the **prefix** that would make this word an opposite – **agree**.

◯ *un-* ◯ *im-* ◯ *mis-* ◯ *dis-*

6 Shade the bubble that shows a word with a **suffix**.

◯ truthful ◯ truth ◯ untruth ◯ true

7 Shade the bubble with the **prefix** that would make this word an opposite – **possible**.

○ *un-* ○ *im-* ○ *mis-* ○ *dis-*

8 Shade the bubble that shows the correct **direct speech** for the following:

Alice asked the Caterpillar why he was wearing such a funny hat.

○ Why are you wearing such a funny hat Mr C

○ "Why are you wearing such a funny hat Mr C?" asked Alice.

○ "Alice," asked Mr C "Why he was wearing such a funny hat."

○ "Why are you wearing such a funny hat Mr C asked Alice?"

9 Shade the bubble that shows the correct **coordinating conjunction** for the following:

Why did the computer go to the doctor? Because it had a virus ________ *needed a check-up!*

○ and ○ but ○ or

10 Shade the bubble that shows the correct **antonym** for the following:

What would the opposite word be for a turtle who is very slow?

○ fast ○ sleepy ○ quiet

How am I doing?

Colour the boxes if you understand.

Quoted or direct speech shows the words that are actually spoken. ☐

Prepositional phrases can tell us where something is happening. ☐

Homophones are words that sound the same but look different and have different meanings. For example: *rode/road, blue/blew* ☐

Time to reflect

Colour each box when you can do the following things.

- ☐ I can use common nouns and proper nouns.
- ☐ I choose suitable nouns in my writing to represent different characters. For example: **girl**, **orphan**, **prince**
- ☐ I can use pronouns to represent people, places, animals, things or ideas.
- ☐ I can use adjectives to describe characters and settings to make my writing more interesting.
- ☐ I know how to use articles and adjectives to make more interesting noun groups.
- ☐ I use verbs in every sentence I write.
- ☐ I use thinking and feeling verbs in my writing.
- ☐ I use lots of different saying verbs in my writing to show the way someone is talking.
- ☐ I know how to use relating verbs (being and having verbs) when I am writing facts in descriptions and reports.
- ☐ I can use present, past and future tense verbs correctly.
- ☐ I use adverbs to tell more about the verbs in my sentences.
- ☐ I use modal verbs such as **could**, **would**, **should** and **must** when expressing opinions.
- ☐ I add phrases to my writing to give details such as **where**, **when**, **how** or **why** something is happening.
- ☐ I understand that some words have opposites (antonyms).
- ☐ I understand that some words have similar meanings (synonyms).
- ☐ I use paragraphs to organise my writing into logical bundles.
- ☐ I sometimes use rhythm, alliteration or onomatopoeia to make my imaginative text writing more interesting or playful.
- ☐ I know how to use the coordinating conjunctions **and**, **but**, **or** and **so** to write longer sentences.
- ☐ I understand that the subject and verb in a sentence must agree.
- ☐ I use capital letters to begin sentences, to write the pronoun *I*, and when I write proper nouns.
- ☐ I use commas in lists and know when to use full stops, question marks and exclamation marks.
- ☐ I understand that an apostrophe of contraction is used to show where a letter is missing in a shortened word.
- ☐ I understand the difference between informative, imaginative and persuasive texts.
- ☐ I understand that some texts look and/or sound the same (homonyms).

Glossary

adjective	A word that describes nouns: *red, old, large, round, three*
adverb	A word that adds meaning, usually to a verb, to tell when, where or how something happens: *slowly, immediately, soon, here*
alliteration	A group of words that begin with or contain the same sound: *seven silly sausages*
antonym	An opposite: *full/empty, sitting/standing, front/back*
article	The words *a, an* and *the*
apostrophe of contraction	A punctuation mark that shows where letters are missing in a shortened word: *isn't, we'll, I'm, shouldn't*
capital letter	An upper-case letter: *ABCDEFGHIJKLMNOPQRSTUVWXYZ*
comma	A punctuation mark that shows a short break or pause in a sentence, separates words in a list or separates parts of a sentence.
coordinating conjunction	A joining word used to join two simple sentences or main ideas: *and, but, or, so*
exclamation	A sentence that shows a raised voice or strong feeling: *Look out!*
exclamation mark	The mark (!) that shows where an exclamation ends.
full stop	The mark (.) that shows where a statement ends: *Zoe is at school.*
homophone	A word that sounds the same but is spelled differently: *sun/son*
main clause	A simple sentence or main idea that always contains a subject and a verb and makes sense by itself.
noun	A word that names people, places, animals, things or ideas. Nouns can be: **abstract nouns** (things that cannot be seen or touched): *happiness* **common nouns** (names of ordinary things): *hat, toys, pet, mouse, clock, bird* **concrete nouns** (things that can be seen or touched): *book, pet, boy, girl* **proper nouns** (special names): *Max, Perth, Friday, March, Grand Final* **technical nouns** (sometimes called scientific nouns): *oxygen*
noun group	A group of words, often including an article, an adjective and a noun, that tell us more about a main noun: *the strange old house*
onomatopoeia	Words that sound like the thing they are describing: *Bang! Crash!*
paragraph	A section of text containing a number of sentences about a particular point. Each paragraph starts on a new line.
phrase	A group of words that adds details about when, where, how, why: *the car, after lunch, with a spoon, for Olivia*
plural	More than one: *chairs, dishes, boxes, cities, donkeys, loaves, fungi*
prefix	A group of letters added to the beginning of a word to change the meaning: *dis*appear, *mis*behave

Glossary *continued*

preposition	A word that usually begins a phrase: *on, in, over, under, before*
prepositional phrase	A phrase that always begins with a preposition: *on the shelf, in the car, over the hill, under the bridge*
pronoun	A word that can take the place of a noun to represent people, places, animals, things or ideas: *he, she, I, it, they, we, us, me, they, them, mine*
punctuation	Special symbols or marks, such as a comma or full stop, that show a pause or break in a sentence
question	A sentence that asks something: *Is Tock hiding under the bed?*
question mark	A question mark (**?**) goes at the end of a question. *What is your name?*
quoted (direct) speech	The words that someone actually says. Quoted speech uses speech marks (quotation marks) at the start and end of the actual words spoken.
rhythm	A regular beat or pattern of sounds or words used in music or poetry.
sentence	A group of words that makes sense and includes a subject and at least one verb. A **simple sentence** has one main idea and one verb or verb group: *The birds were sitting on the fence.* A **compound sentence** uses *and, but, or, so* to join two main ideas. A compound sentence has two verbs or verb groups: *Some birds were sitting on the fence and a cat was lurking below.*
statement	A sentence that states facts or gives opinions: *The horses ran around the paddock. I like ice cream.*
subject	The noun or noun group naming who or what a sentence is about.
suffix	A group of letters added to the end of a word. Suffixes often change the function of a word: *smile* (noun) – *smiling* (verb)
synonym	A word that means the same or nearly the same as another word: *shouts/ yells, thin/skinny*
topic sentence	A sentence, usually placed at the start of a paragraph, that introduces the main point being made in the paragraph.
verb	A word that tells us what is happening in a sentence. Verbs can be: **doing verbs**: *walked, swam* **saying verbs**: *said, asked* **thinking and feeling verbs**: *know, like* **relating verbs**: *am, is, are, had* **modal verbs** (telling how sure we are about doing something): *should, could, would, may, might, must, can, will, shall*
verb group	A group of words that tells us more about a main verb: *might have been wondering* (in this example, *wondering* is the main verb)
verb tense	The form a verb takes to show when an action takes place – in the present, past or future: *runs/is running, thought/was thinking, will help*